MW00563510

HARRY STYLES IS LIFE

HARRY STYLES IS LIFE

A Superfan's Guide to All Things We Love about Harry Styles

KATHLEEN PERRICONE

ILLUSTRATED BY JESSICA DURRANT

CONTENTS

INTRODUCTION

It's all love!

What you see is what you get with Harry Styles: beautiful inside and out, the singer is as genuine as his smile, as confident as his avant-garde fashion, and as passionate as his love songs. According to the person who's known Harry his entire life, his mother, Anne Twist, "He's just the same as he has always been." She told the *Daily Mail* in 2023: "As a very little boy, he was very much like he is now, just a smaller version."

Harry's authenticity as an artist and a human is what gravitates millions of faithful Stylers toward him. An overnight sensation from the moment he first appeared on *The X Factor* as a teen in 2010, he evolved from One Direction (1D)'s goofy heartthrob into one of the most successful solo acts on the planet, with a fanbase that spans all ages. Harry's an old soul through and through. Heavily influenced by the sounds of the 1960s and '70s—Fleetwood Mac, David Bowie, the Beatles, the Rolling Stones, and Pink Floyd—his three chart-topping albums incorporated classic rock elevated with a modern edge that appeals to Generations X, Y, Z, and even baby boomers.

Millions have come out to his shows to sing and dance like no one's watching.

Inclusion is a tenet of Harry's ideology, and his concerts have earned a reputation for providing a safe space for everyone, free of any judgment. Millions have come out to his shows to sing and dance like no one's watching and many have been inspired to literally come out. Most recently, during a stop on the Australian leg of Harry's Love On Tour, the sixth-highest-grossing tour of all time ($617.3 million), a female fan named Fauve caught the singer's attention. She held up a sign asking him to help tell her parents, who were in attendance, that she was gay. Harry made the moment extra special with coming-out music as he led a sing-along of fifty-six thousand people at Melbourne's

Marvel Stadium. "Rise to the heavens of freedom," he told Fauve, who was embraced by her tearful mother. "Enjoy yourself!"

Harry's broad-minded approach has blown open doors for himself as well. In 2020, he became the first ever solo male to grace the cover of *Vogue*—wearing a dress, no less. The historic fashion moment redefined masculinity, a polarizing achievement met with equal amounts of controversy and celebration. But the opinions of the outside world never had an adverse effect on his own universe.

"That's my Harry," gushed his childhood idol turned confidante, Fleetwood Mac singer Stevie Nicks. "I think the thing that's most wonderful about him . . . is that he's such a kooky guy. He's the type of person you'd wanna live next door to. He'd look out the window, see you having a hard time planting flowers, and rush out asking, 'Can I help you with those roses?' . . . That's who he is."

PART ONE

Story of His Life

165998

FOREVER YOUNG

From the moment he was born on February 1, 1994, Harry Edward Styles charmed almost everyone. With just a bat of his baby blue eyes or a cheeky grin, hearts melted. Even in nursery school, his adoring teacher played favorites. "I probably got to play with the good toys more than the other kids," the self-proclaimed mommy's boy joked in *Dare to Dream: Life as One Direction*. As he got a little older, he discovered his magic also worked on girls his age.

At age six, Harry made his first move when he bought a teddy bear for his crush, Phoebe, whom he described as "the cutest little girl." At seven, "he particularly excelled in the schmoozing game," recalled his elder sister, Gemma Anne Styles. During a family vacation in Cyprus, "he was holding court around the pool with people three times his age." They were so smitten that when the Styles family left to go home to England, the young women gathered on the sidewalk to see him off at the airport shuttle. "Bye, Harry, we love you," they shouted as he waved back to his earliest fans. "He just had this unbelievable way with girls all his life," childhood friend Will Sweeney told the UK's *Daily Star*. "I know it sounds funny, but even in primary school he had a few girls on the go."

Harry's other love was performing in school plays. When he was five, he stole the show as Barney, a singing mouse who lived in a church. "I had to wear a pair of my sister's gray tights and a headband with ears on and sing in front of everyone," he recounted in 1D's 2011 autobiography. "I like to think I was a good mouse." Fans would agree—a minute-long clip of young Harry onstage confidently singing and acting out the lyrics gained hundreds of thousands of views on YouTube. The top comment deemed it "the cutest video in history."

His second performance was a role created just for him: Buzz Lightyear in a stage adaptation of *Chitty Chitty Bang Bang*. Although the *Toy Story* superhero was not in the 1968 fantasy musical, his teacher added him to a *Chitty Chitty Bang Bang* scene set in a toy store. Similarly, Harry originated his character in his school's cast for *Joseph and the Amazing Technicolor Dreamcoat*: "I was the pharaoh, but I was an Elvis pharaoh," he told *Rolling Stone* in 2012. "I think I just knew I wanted to entertain people and stuff. I was a bit of an attention-seeker at school."

"I had to wear a pair of my sister's gray tights and a headband with ears on and sing in front of everyone."

At home, Harry was just as animated, and this brought a smile to his mother's face in the toughest of times. Growing up in the sleepy village of Holmes Chapel (population: 5,000), he and Anne were very close, and after she divorced Harry's father, Desmond Styles, their bond deepened.

Harry was seven when his parents sat him and Gemma down and revealed they were splitting. "It was the worst day of my life," Desmond recalled to *People* in 2012. "[Harry] wasn't a crybaby or generally emotional, but he cried then . . . Everybody was in tears." Desmond eventually moved out and found a place about thirty miles (48 km) away in Manchester—still close enough to see Harry every few weeks. Anne took Harry and Gemma to live further into the Cheshire countryside, where she found work as a bartender.

When Harry was nine, his mother remarried a local pub owner named John Cox, yet it was short-lived. "Since I've been ten, it's kind of felt like—protect Mom at all costs," Harry revealed to *Rolling Stone* in 2017. "My mom is very strong. She has the greatest heart." And so does her son, according to Gemma. "When she'd had a bad day, as we all do sometimes, we tried to step up where we could," she wrote in a 2017 essay for *Another Man*. "Harry's attempts at cheering her up were all the better for their youthful earnestness. A twelve-year-old has seen enough romcoms to know that a thoughtful bloke is one who runs a bath, so that's what she'd get from time to time, with a mismatch of house-gathered candles placed around the bathroom."

The Styles siblings couldn't have been more different, yet their personalities complement each other: What one lacked, it seemed the other made up for in spades. Introverted Gemma, who was three years older than Harry, excelled in school and dreamed of becoming a teacher. At home, she practiced with her little brother, who pretended to be a student, even using different voices during roll call. But for Harry, learning didn't come as easily.

When he joined Gemma at Holmes Chapel Comprehensive School, a secondary school, former teachers would comment, "So . . . I met your brother." "I was geeky, quiet and, I guess, pretty easy to have in class," noted Gemma. "[Harry's] a joker, talkative and very distracting—not ideal for a productive lesson." When his mediocre grades didn't match his sister's, he would get frustrated. However, instead of teasing him, Gemma helped Harry with his science and English studies and prepped him for exams. "I could never fathom how he had a confidence problem; he was popular, decent at sports, and not a bad student either," she wrote in *Another Man*. "I would have traded my As for his Bs and charisma in a heartbeat."

"If it didn't work out, then fair enough, but if I didn't try I'd never know."

But there was one thing that made Harry shy. Although he had unabashedly performed in school plays as a little boy, he only sang around the house as he got older, usually playing with the karaoke machine he got from his grandfather. But word got around Holmes Chapel that Harry had talent.

In 2009, a group of friends approached the fifteen-year-old about joining their band. They wanted to enter a school competition and needed a vocalist. It was a dream come true for Harry, although he questioned his skills as a frontman. "Harry didn't think he could sing and was worried people would laugh," bassist Nick Clough told *Sunday Mirror*. "There was a born performer in there, he just had to find it. But when his confidence grew, he was amazing." The teen band took on the name White Eskimo, a term referring to native people from the Arctic regions that has since been deemed derogatory.

After weeks of rehearsals, by the time of the Battle of the Bands, the quartet—a guitarist, bassist, drummer, and Harry on the tambourine—was a polished unit. All dressed in white shirts with black ties, they electrified the school cafeteria with covers of Jet's "Are You Gonna Be My Girl" and "Summer of '69" by Bryan Adams and won first place.

Harry's innate ability to win over female fans was already obvious at his very first gig: After the show, an awestruck girl approached the teen as if she had just witnessed the second coming of Mick Jagger or Freddie Mercury. "Where did that come from?" she gushed. "The crowd loved him," remembered Nick. "Harry's showmanship made the band."

Their second gig was one that paid: A girl at school asked White Eskimo to perform at her mother's wedding for £40 ($50) each and free sandwiches. The band rehearsed twenty-five songs requested by the bride, including several by Bob Marley, "and it all went really well," Harry recounted in *Dare to Dream*. "One of the guests at the wedding was a music producer, and afterward he came and spoke to us and told us we were really good. He also said that I reminded him of Mick Jagger, which of course I loved."

But did Harry have what it took to be as successful as the Rolling Stones singer? He wasn't convinced. At sixteen, he passed his GCSEs (General Certificate of Secondary Education exams), which would allow him to move on to college where he hoped to study law, sociology, and business, and one day become a physiotherapist. "But I wanted to see if I could make it as a singer first," Harry revealed in *One Direction: Forever Young: Our Official X Factor Story* (HarperCollins, 2011). "If it didn't work out, then fair enough, but if I didn't try I'd never know."

On Saturdays, Harry and Nick worked at the W. Mandeville Bakery in their hometown, earning £6 ($7.60) an hour. One day, Harry was in the back sweeping "and singing really loud because he thought no one was in the shop," recalled Nick. "A customer came in and asked, 'Who's singing?' I brought Harry out and the customer said, 'Have you ever thought about singing professionally?'"

Of course he had, but nerves kept him from taking the leap—so his mother gave him a gentle shove. In early 2010, Anne signed up her sixteen-year-old son to audition on *The X Factor*, the music competition show created by *American Idol* judge Simon Cowell. "I was watching the year before, and I remember looking at the young guys on there—and I was kind of like, 'I'd love to have a go at it just to see what happens,' and that was kind of it," Harry told *Rolling Stone* in 2012. "My mum actually did the application. And then three weeks later, I walked upstairs, and she said, 'Oh, you've got your *X Factor* audition Sunday,' and I was like, 'OK.'"

Anne and Gemma helped Harry pick his audition songs, but when it came time to practice, "he suddenly became shy and wouldn't let us listen," recalled his sister. "After a lot of persuasion, he would stand in the bathroom with the door shut and sing [Stevie Wonder's] "Isn't She Lovely" and "Hey, Soul Sister" [by Train], while Mum and I sat on the landing outside. I'd never experienced a shy Harry, and never honestly appreciated that he could really sing—it was usually hidden behind humor or sarcasm or some silly voice . . . As soon as it was serious, and he was being himself, it was like he'd had his shield snatched away. And he was great."

LIKE FATHER, LIKE SON

Harry's bond with his father has always been over their love of music. As a kid, he was introduced to Desmond Styles' classic-rock favorites like the Beatles, Fleetwood Mac, the Rolling Stones, and Queen. At six, Harry learned the words to another one of his father's recommendations, Elvis Presley's "The Girl of My Best Friend," which he recorded on a karaoke machine. There were also some things he was too young to understand, particularly Pink Floyd's *The Dark Side of the Moon,* a 1973 concept album that explored greed, death, and mental illness. "I couldn't really get it," Harry confessed to *Rolling Stone,* "but I just remember being like, 'This is really fucking cool.'" These early influences stuck with Desmond's son, who paid homage to his father's favorite bands on his solo debut album and even gave him an exclusive preview. Desmond especially loved "Carolina," an energetic rock song brought to life with a sing-along chorus of "la la la" reminiscent of the Beatles.

TEEN DREAM

Harry's family and friends thought he had the "X Factor"—but would professional talent scouts agree? In July 2010, the sixteen-year-old traveled to neighboring Manchester with his mother, sister, stepfather, and friends in tow to audition for the reality competition. The judging panel was led by Simon Cowell, who was named one of the most influential people in the world that year by *TIME* magazine.

Standing before the crowd at Manchester Central convention complex, Harry didn't show a hint of nervousness as he affably bantered with Cowell, who initially seemed more annoyed than charmed by the floppy-haired teen. Why was Harry auditioning for *The X Factor*, he wanted to know? "My mum's always told me that I'm a good singer . . ." Harry replied. Cowell rolled his eyes. "Okay, mums normally don't know," he said with a laugh. "I think I could do it," countered Harry, "but with your help, I could be a lot better." It was the moment of truth.

Harry sang "Hey Soul Sister," smiling as he worked the stage to engage with the audience. After only twenty seconds, Cowell cut the music. The performance was off, so he asked Harry to sing something else, a cappella. Without hesitation, the teen launched into "Isn't She Lovely." The judges were impressed: Nicole Scherzinger of the Pussycat Dolls said he had "a beautiful voice"; Irish music manager Louis Walsh agreed, but felt Harry didn't have enough "confidence" due to his young age. The crowd reacted strongly, as did Cowell. "Someone in the audience just said 'rubbish' and I totally agree with them," he remarked, bringing a smile back to Harry's face. "I think with a bit of vocal coaching you actually could be very good." Cowell and Scherzinger voted "yes" to send Harry to the next round while Walsh's lone "no" was thoroughly booed by the crowd.

Weeks later, Harry was summoned to *The X Factor Boot Camp* for professional training. It was the first time the teen had ever been to London, three hours south of Holmes Chapel. However, his mother couldn't get time off from work. Gemma, home from college for the summer, volunteered to go with her little brother and turned the experience into a sightseeing adventure. The siblings visited the Natural History Museum and Harrods department store before taking the train

"None of us wanted him to fail but we never dreamed things would go the way they did."

to Wembley Stadium for round two of the competition. "Everyone looked so much older than him," Gemma recalled. "Sixteen years old and in the shadows of a building we'd only seen on TV. I stayed nearby so that when the call came and he was out of the competition, I could go and commiserate, take him home to Cheshire and school, and back to his normal life. None of us wanted him to fail but we never dreamed things would go the way they did."

Harry sailed through the first challenge of boot camp with a group vocal performance of Michael Jackson's "Man in the Mirror." But his solo number fell flat, and he was among the handful of male contestants who didn't make it through to the next round. Backstage, cameras caught a heartbroken Harry wiping away tears with his knit beanie.

"I think you're the next big boy band."

As he prepared for the long trip back to Holmes Chapel—and a mundane life studying for his A levels and working at the bakery on Saturdays—the judges requested that Harry, along with four other rejected boys, return to the stage. "We thought of each of you as individuals, and we just feel you're too talented to let go of," teased Scherzinger. Instead, the judges decided to group the five into one boy band and advance them to the next round. Harry, overcome with emotion, dropped to his knees and was embraced by his new bandmates Niall Horan, Zayn Malik, Liam Payne, and Louis Tomlinson. The quintet chose the name One Direction, which Harry suggested, as it reflected their collective mindset to go straight to the top of the competition.

The X Factor is formatted in such a way that, after boot camp and before the live shows, each judge mentors eight contestants who spend a week at their home practicing for the next elimination round. One Direction was assigned to Cowell—who lived in Spain. With only a few days to go before Cowell was expecting them, the boys used the time to get to know one another. Harry invited everyone to his mother's house, where Anne and her live-in boyfriend Robin Twist stocked the refrigerator "and lef us to our own devices," he recalled in *Dare to Dream*. "I cooked dinner for us one night—chicken breasts, fries, and peas—and we all sat around the table in the bungalow talking rubbish. Other than that, I think we ate Super Noodles most days." Admittedly, 1D goofed off more than they rehearsed, "but it was a really good way of getting to know each other's personalities." Harry especially got along with eighteen-year-old Louis, who grew up seventy miles (113 km) away in South Yorkshire and worked a series of odd jobs before auditioning for *The X Factor*. The two were similar, he noted, in that they're both funny yet know when to "go into serious mode."

At Cowell's compound in Spain, 1D amazed their mentor with a perfectly harmonized rendition of Natalie Imbruglia's "Torn." The usually stoic Cowell gushed, "They're cool, they're relevant." When the group debuted on live TV that October, they had the same effect on the voting audience—which at fourteen million was the highest ratings in the show's seven-year history.

Each week, 1D held steady at the top of the competition, buoyed by their performances of "Total Eclipse of the Heart," "Kids in America," and "Summer of '69"—the same song that helped White Eskimo win the Battle of the Bands. As they approached the semifinals, however, Harry woke up one morning "feeling properly awful" with a throat infection. He slept through one rehearsal and was at the doctor's office for another. He bounced back in time for the big night when 1D proved how much they'd evolved over the competition. "I think you're the next big boy band," praised Walsh after their polished performance of "Chasing Cars" by alternative rock band, Snow Patrol. "All the young kids are going to lift the phones and they're going to vote One Direction into the final because you deserve it."

Fans did indeed flood *The X Factor* hotline, securing 1D the third spot in the two-part finale. But although they dazzled the judges with Elton John's "Your Song" the first night, their encore performance of "Torn" wasn't enough to beat their competition. As the five took one last bow, Harry was visibly gutted. "What would happen to One Direction?" asked *The X Factor* host Dermot O'Leary. "We're definitely going to stay together," replied Zayn with a wink. Although the group didn't win *The X Factor*, they ultimately earned the same prize: A record deal with Cowell's Syco Music. Weeks after the show's finale, *The Sun* reported 1D had signed a £2-million ($2.5 million) deal and would be the label's top priority in 2011. "Simon is keen to get One Direction cracking," a source told the British newspaper. "[They] will put out a first single this spring. Then hear the cash register chime."

FAN FAVORITE

With its five good-looking members, One Direction had a heartthrob for everyone. But from the onset, Harry emerged as the most popular among fans. The adoration started from the moment of his debut on *The X Factor*—the very next day, he was recognized at a gas station. Throughout the show's run, anytime 1D headed for rehearsals, fans lined up outside adorned with posters of their favorite group member. After the live show on week 6, Harry was reportedly caught with a teenage fan in Simon Cowell's dressing room. According to *The Mirror*, "Harry is like a kid in a candy store. He has thousands of girls sending him fan mail every week." By the show's finale, Harry was one of the most famous faces in the UK. In December 2010, months after *The X Factor*'s premiere, the mop-topped teen was voted Best Celebrity Hair in a poll conducted by *NOW* magazine—beating out Prince Harry.

BEST BOY BAND EVER

With millions of fans anxiously awaiting their debut album, One Direction was poised to skyrocket to superstardom. In November 2011, nearly a year since their final bow on *The X Factor*, the boy band released *Up All Night*, which shot right to the top of the charts in sixteen countries and sold 4.5 million copies, boosted by lead single "What Makes You Beautiful." Harry knew it would be a hit the moment he heard the demo. A "fun" track with a catchy hook, "it kind of represented us," he told

MTV News. So did the music video, which showed the guys enjoying a beach day in Malibu and introduced 1D to a global audience who hadn't watched their UK reality show. It was love at first sight for new fans: the group's first world tour sold out within minutes in the UK, US, and Australia.

After wrapping up fifty-four concerts, there would be no rest for Harry, Liam, Niall, Louis, and Zayn. They performed at the 2012 Summer Olympics closing ceremony in London, then jetted off to New York for the *MTV Video Music Awards*, where they were the big winners of the night with three trophies for Best New Artist, Best Pop Video, and Most Share-Worthy Video. The most impressive fact for these newbies is that they had beat out the likes of Beyoncé, Justin Bieber, Rihanna, and Maroon 5. Their meteoric success was unprecedented—but was it sustainable? Harry was honest about his anxiety concerning 1D's destiny. "We're just excited most of the time and having so much fun," he told *Rolling Stone*. "I think you have to enjoy it while it's going on. I think you should be wary about the future, but not worrying about it all the time."

Syco Music decided to strike while the iron was hot: Twelve months after 1D's first album, they released their follow-up, *Take Me Home*, which debuted at the top of the *Billboard* 200 chart, making 1D the first boy band ever to record two No.1 albums in a single calendar year. Several tracks were written by up-and-coming hitmaker Ed Sheeran, including "Little Things," a pop ballad about loving someone's imperfections that became a popular first dance song at weddings.

While some critics saw *Take Me Home* as a cash grab to capitalize on 1D's fifteen minutes of fame, Harry explained it was to showcase the group's growth as harmonizing vocalists in real time. "I think on the first album there are a few tracks where you can tell we're still kind of trying to find out what the One Direction sound is," he told MTV News. "This time we kind of know what it is and we can kind of focus on that. We think the songs are better on this album," which he described as "next level" compared to *Up All Night*.

In early 2013, 1D embarked on their first all-arena tour: a whopping 134 shows throughout North America, Europe, Asia, and Oceania, including six sold-out nights at London's O2 arena. Any free moment the guys had was spent in a recording studio working on their third album, *Midnight Memories*, a collection of songs more rock than pop—thanks to Harry's influence. The nineteen-year-old cowrote a handful of the tracks, including "Right Now" with OneRepublic's Ryan Tedder and "Something Great" with Gary Lightbody of Snow Patrol. Released just five weeks before the end of 2013, *Midnight Memories* became the best-selling album of the year with four million copies sold, due in part to the biggest singles in 1D's brief history, "Best Song Ever" and "Story of My Life."

The making of *Midnight Memories* was documented by Academy Award–nominee Morgan Spurlock, the filmmaker who famously ate at McDonald's for thirty days in *Super Size Me*. *One Direction: This Is Us* gave fans an all-access look at the world's most popular boy band as they juggled their personal and professional lives. Harry admitted it was "nerve-racking" to allow a stranger to film his every move, but ultimately, he trusted Spurlock's vision to capture their true personalities. For Harry, a big part of that was about where he's from, so the cameras followed him back to Holmes Chapel.

The footage revealed that the pop star was no different from the average teenager, raiding his family's refrigerator and sleeping until noon. It showed Harry paying a visit to the bakery where he had gotten his first job at the age of fourteen. It was like no time had passed at all as he slipped on an apron (and snuck cookies from the display case). "He's got this aura of charm about him," owner Simon Wakefield reminisced about his most famous employee. Harry also reunited with a former coworker named Barbara "who used to pinch my bum every Saturday." After the box office success of *This Is Us*, fans would make pilgrimages to W. Mandeville Bakery specifically to interrogate the older woman about Harry's backside.

The 1D phenomenon made history in 2013 when they became the first boy band to gross $1 billion. Only three years after their formation on *The X Factor*, the quintet were inescapable, with chart-topping albums, sold-out world tours, best-selling autobiographies, a blockbuster documentary, and even their own action figures. Reflecting on the fast-tracked superstardom in *One Direction: Where We Are: Our Band, Our Story: 100% Official* (HarperCollins, 2013), Harry admitted it could be "intrusive" at times, but he has tried to focus on the positive aspects of fame, particularly traveling the world and making memories with four of his closest friends. Among the highlights were meeting First Lady Michelle Obama, performing at Madison Square Garden, doing charity work in Ghana, and stealing a pink bar of soap from Johnny Depp's bathroom.

The exhausting grind didn't stop as 2014 brought 1D's fourth album and world tour in as many years. But had the boy band oversaturated the market? *Four* debuted at No. 1 in eighteen countries. However, it only sold half as many copies as *Midnight Memories*. Still, One Direction mania

The footage revealed that the pop star was no different from the average teenager, raiding his family's refrigerator and sleeping until noon.

was at an all-time high as the sold-out On the Road Again tour kicked off in February 2015. Just weeks later, however, Zayn abruptly quit the band "because I want to be a normal twenty-two-year-old who is able to relax and have some private time out of the spotlight," he said in an official statement. "I know I have four friends for life in Louis, Liam, Harry, and Niall." And they would carry on as a quartet, much to the relief of Directioners everywhere. "We're looking forward to recording the new album and seeing all the fans on the next stage of the world tour," 1D announced.

In July 2015, fans got their first listen of the Zayn-less One Direction with the pop-rock single "Drag Me Down," a surprise release that broke the record for most streams in a day on Spotify at 4.75 million. Critics praised 1D's more "mature" sound, as did Zayn himself. "Proud of my boys the new single is sick," he wrote on Twitter (now known as X), the same week he had signed a solo deal with RCA Records. Although it seemed like the beginning of 1D as a quartet, it was actually the end of the boy band altogether. Weeks later, they confirmed reports that they were taking a "hiatus" after five nonstop years and would not tour behind their forthcoming album, *Made in the A.M.*

As rumors swirled about their future, the four members put up a united front at the *American Music Awards*, where they won Artist of the Year to close out 2015—and perhaps their time as a group. In January 2016, it was reported that 1D had not renewed their contracts and the split would be permanent. Although representatives for the group denied it was true, it's been nearly a decade later and 1D has yet to return from their hiatus.

Harry has never shut the door on a reunion. Over the years, he's been asked several times about this, and most recently on *The Late Late Show with James Corden* in 2023. "I think I would never say never to that," he replied. "If there was a time when we wanted to do it, I don't see why we wouldn't."

THE FAB FIVE

Not since the Beatles has a band caused such global mania as One Direction. Comparisons between the Fab Four and 1D were immediately made during week 3 of *The X Factor*, when the teens were mobbed by hundreds of screaming fans while out shopping. As the group officially launched post–*X Factor*, they studied the original idols by watching a film about their historic 1964 arrival in America. "To be honest, that really was like us," said Harry. "Stepping off the plane, the girls, the madness . . . Fame-wise, it's probably even bigger." Paul McCartney addressed the notion that 1D was "the next Beatles" in 2012, calling the comparison "the kiss of death" for any band, given the high expectations. The following year, he admitted, "I like One Direction," to the *Wall Street Journal* and noted the parallels with his legendary band. "They're young, beautiful boys and that's the big attraction. But they can sing, they make good records."

A NEW DIRECTION

As Harry prepared for life after One Direction, he began laying the groundwork for a solo career. The day before the boy band's final performance on New Year's Eve 2015, the *Telegraph* reported that the twenty-one-year-old had registered eight songs with the American Society of Composers, Authors and Publishers (ASCAP). The songs had been cowritten with Snow Patrol singer Gary Lightbody and guitarist Johnny McDaid as well as Gary Go, a producer best known for his work with Rihanna and Kylie Minogue.

"He's a rare breed, a truly cool, magnetic personality."

As fans buzzed about Harry's next move, he took a major step forward in June 2016 when he signed a deal with Columbia Records. Much to his surprise, it didn't include a "cleanliness clause" like his 1D contract, which had allowed Cowell's label to drop him if he did anything deemed unacceptable. At the realization, Harry burst into tears. "I felt free," he confessed to *Better Homes and Gardens*.

To ensure Columbia wouldn't control the direction of his album, Harry called the CEO of Sony Music Entertainment (which owns the label), Rob Stringer, and conveyed to him, "I kind of need to figure this out a little bit . . . and I'm not going to be able to do it if you're breathing down my neck," Harry recounted on *The Howard Stern Show*. Stringer wholeheartedly agreed. "Go do your thing," he told the artist. "And when you're ready, I'll hear it."

Without restrictions, Harry began working on his solo debut, with "honesty" as his theme. "I didn't want to write 'stories'; I wanted to write *my* stories, things that happened to me," he explained to *Rolling Stone* in 2017. "I hadn't done that before." It was also the first time he got to make decisions about his music not as part of a democracy. As he figured out the sound he wanted to create—one heavily influenced by 1970s classic rock—he met with several pop hitmakers, including singer Bruno Mars and producer Max Martin, who worked on Taylor Swift's *1989* and Katy Perry's *Teenage Dream*. On the opposite end of the spectrum, he booked a meeting with Jeff Bhasker, best known for working with Kanye West, Lana Del Rey, and the Rolling Stones. "I didn't have many notions about what to do with him," Bhasker admitted to *Hits* magazine. "When he told me what he wanted to do, I said, 'OK, wow—you wanna have an actual rock band.' After meeting him, I experienced what a special vibe he has—he's a rare breed, a truly cool, magnetic personality."

Los Angeles–based Bhasker enlisted two musical friends to help Harry form "a cool indie band" before they could begin the recording process. When one of the prospective guitarists didn't show, engineer Ryan Nasci brought in his roommate Mitch Rowland, a dishwasher who had never stepped foot in a studio—nor even heard of Harry Styles before. "The second he plugged in his guitar and started playing, Harry's eyes just lit up and he was, like, 'This is the guy,'" recalled Bhasker. Within a week, the singer and his band had written ten songs. "I listened to them, and my response was, 'This is not necessarily the pop hit No. 1 smash Harry song out of the gate,' where a lot of my pop brain kicked in," said Bhasker. "Then, after I listened to them for a while, I was just, like, 'But I *love* this—I wanna *listen* to this.'" So did Directioners, who transformed into Stylers once the former boybander dropped his first single as a solo artist in April 2017. "Sign of the Times," a pop-rock power ballad about "the state of the world," shot right to the top of the charts.

Critics were equally impressed: *Billboard* noted it showed Harry's range as an artist as he stepped "boldly away from the manufactured, plastic pop of his past"; *Rolling Stone* ranked "Sign of the Times" the best song of the year. The music video symbolizes Harry's risk appetite: In the cinematic

visual, he flies high over Scotland's picturesque Isle of Skye without green-screen or computer-generated imagery (CGI) effects (except, of course, for the ending when he floats up into the heavens). Paparazzi photos of the shoot show the superstar suspended more than a thousand feet (305 m) from a helicopter, the cables digitally erased post-production. For his death-defying stunts, Harry earned Video of the Year at the *BRIT Awards* and *iHeartRadio Music Awards*, as well as two nominations at the *MTV Video Music Awards*. And as of 2024, "Sign of the Times" has 1.2 billion views on YouTube—more than any other One Direction video.

Harry's solo debut album, *Harry Styles*, is a true reflection of who he is as an artist, with songs of love and heartbreak rooted in the kind of music he had listened to growing up, but with a modern twist. Critics easily identified his biggest influences: Pink Floyd, the Rolling Stones, the Beatles, David Bowie, and Fleetwood Mac.

But why take such a risk when he's only been known as a pop star? "That's just what my references are," he admitted to the *New York Times*. "A lot of people, when they make music, they build a wall between them and fans. They think: 'We'll do this because people will get it.' I really wanted to make an album that I wanted to listen to. That was the only way I knew I wouldn't look back on it and regret it. It was more, 'What do I want to sit and listen to?' rather than, 'How do I shake up compared to what's on the radio right now?'"

A commercial and critical success, *Harry Styles* could have been an epic flop, and he still would have been proud of what he created coming off the "roller coaster" of One Direction. Reminiscing about the first time he played it for his parents, "There was something about . . . how happy I was that told them, 'If all I get is to make this music, I'm content. If I'm never on that big ride again, I'm happy and proud of it.'"

WHERE ARE THEY NOW?

In the decade since One Direction went in five separate directions, the guys have all achieved their own levels of solo success. To Harry, that speaks of how dedicated they had been in making One Direction the biggest boy band in history. Consequently, he feels that they should be celebrated individually instead of pitted against one another by the media. "We loved being in that band," he told *Variety*. "I think it's never been about that for us. It's about a next step in evolution. The fact that we've all achieved different things outside of the band says a lot about how hard we worked in it."

ZAYN: The first to leave 1D and release a solo album, he's also been the most vocal about his unhappiness while in the boy band. Months after quitting, Zayn revealed to *The Fader* that "there was never any room for me to experiment creatively." He had plenty of freedom on his 2016 solo debut, *Mind of Mine*, an alternative R&B-tinged collection of songs inspired by his life experiences "over the past five years." In the music video for lead single "Pillowtalk," Zayn gave fans an intimate look at life with his new girlfriend, model Gigi Hadid (the two welcomed a daughter in 2020 but split the following year). Many saw his 2016 collaboration with Harry's ex, Taylor Swift, on "I Don't Want to Live Forever" as a dig at his former bandmate, but admittedly Zayn—who put out two more albums that didn't generate much buzz, with the upcoming *Room Under the Stairs*—doesn't maintain any relationships with the 1D guys.

NIALL: The second 1D member to put out solo music, Niall performed his debut single, the folk-pop "This Town," everywhere from *The Ellen Show* to *The Tonight Show Starring Jimmy Fallon* to the 2016 *American Music Awards*. After Harry, he's arguably had the most success in the US, with all three albums debuting on the *Billboard* charts at Nos. 1, 4, and 2 respectively. Irish-born Niall was even invited by President Joe Biden to perform at the White House for St. Patrick's Day in 2023. While in Los Angeles, he found the time to reunite with Harry: Directioners went into a frenzy when a photograph surfaced of Niall walking with someone resembling

Harry whose face was obscured by a mask. "That is Mr. Styles, yes," he confirmed on Capital FM. Not only were they still friends, but also fans of each other's successes. When Harry won the Grammy Award for Album of the Year, Niall posted a photo on Instagram with the caption "very proud."

LOUIS: The 1D member with the least number of vocal solos, Louis stepped into the spotlight on 2016's "Just Hold On," a collaboration with DJ Steve Aoki that he performed on *The X Factor*. The moment was bittersweet: Harry, Liam, and Niall were all in attendance too, as a show of support, because Louis' mother had passed away just days earlier. In 2018, he returned to *The X Factor* as a judge and mentor alongside Simon Cowell, and helped his contestant win Season 15. Two years later, Louis finally released his first solo album, *Walls*, but just as he was set to embark on a world tour, COVID-19 forced him to postpone. Instead, Louis put on a virtual concert for 160,000 people, breaking the Guinness World Record for Most Tickets Sold for a Livestreamed Concert by a Solo Male Artist. He chronicled the making of his second album in *All of Those*

Voices, a documentary about his journey from 1D to solo act that streamed on Paramount+ in the US.

LIAM: Of all the guys in 1D, Liam has probably had the most eclectic post-boy-band trajectory, venturing into electronica and hip-hop. His debut single, "Strip That Down" features Migos rapper Quavo and was released a month after Harry's "Sign of the Times," which Liam admitted he didn't like. "It's not my sort of music, it's not something I'd listen to," he told *Music Choice.* Two years later, he changed his tune when he suggested the duo should collaborate on "a really cool song together" after listening to Harry's *Fine Line.* The timing was interesting: Liam had just released his lone solo album, *LP1*—which peaked at No. 111 on the *Billboard* 200 chart and sold 9,500 copies in its first week. Like Niall, Liam publicly applauded Harry's 2023 Grammy Award. "When you write music like you do, Harry, you deserve every millisecond of that moment looking down, smiling at the trophy you've earned," he wrote on Instagram. "God bless you, brother, congratulations."

HARRY'S WORLD

After introducing himself as a solo artist with *Harry Styles*, Harry shed all traces of his boy band past on *Fine Line*. The success of his debut took the pressure off its follow-up, allowing him the freedom to truly experiment. "When I listen back to the first album now, although I still love it so much, I feel like I was almost bowling with the bumpers up a little bit. I can hear places where I was playing it safe," he revealed to National Public Radio (NPR).

Fans were none the wiser, however: nearly all eighty dates on Harry's Love On Tour sold out. "Ultimately, I think if people believe in you, you can make a bad record, you can make a bad song, and people will still come to a show if they're interested, and they want to come see you. I think the only time people go 'You know what? I'm done with this,' is when it stops being authentic . . . The worst thing that can happen is that I make a record that I think everybody else wants to hear, and then it doesn't do well."

Harry didn't have to worry about that: 2019's *Fine Line* debuted at No. 1 on the *Billboard* 200 chart and went on to sell more than twice its predecessor, with an estimated five million copies to date. For Harry, it was much more than record sales—he had grown as a songwriter. Critics widely praised *Fine Line* as his "most soulful" material. Stevie Nicks, his childhood idol-turned-friend, compared the album to *Rumours*, her band Fleetwood Mac's 1977 magnum opus that sold forty million copies. "Harry writes and sings his songs about real experiences that seemingly happened yesterday," Nicks told *Variety*. "He taps into real life. He doesn't make up stories. He tells the truth, and that is what I do."

Harry described *Fine Line* as "all about having sex and feeling sad." The twenty-five-year-old was coming off a breakup with French model Camille Rowe that had "a big impact on him," revealed producer Kid Harpoon, also one of Harry's closest friends. A handful of songs were inspired by the heartbreak, including "Falling," "Adore You," and "Cherry." The latter, about his jealousy over her new boyfriend, is actually one of Harry's favorites on the album, "mostly because of how it came about," he told NPR. "I was trying this stuff one night in the studio, and I was worried because I just wasn't really liking anything that I was doing. I felt like I was trying too hard."

Around 2 a.m., he took a break and sat down to chat with another producer, Tyler Johnson. Harry went on a tangent about the future, laying out a path of the kind of music he wanted to make in the next five and ten years, "and then I'll get to make the music that I really want to make." And Tyler just said, "You just have to make the music that you want to make—right now. That's the only way of doing it, otherwise you're going to regret it." Harry stayed up the rest of the night recording "Cherry." When he listened back to it, he agreed, "This is the kind of music I want to make."

The buzz around *Fine Line* opened up a new avenue for the solo artist. Harry filled in for James Corden as host of *The Late Late Show*, interviewing himself with some split-screen trickery and playing a round of "Spill Your Guts" with ex-girlfriend Kendall Jenner—during which he opted to eat a giant water scorpion instead of ranking the solo careers of his One Direction bandmates. On *Saturday Night Live*, he pulled double duty as musical guest and host. In his funniest skit, he portrayed a singing chihuahua named Doug. "It was an impressive performance that showed off Styles' comic and acting chops," praised *Variety*, "skills we're sure to see more of in the future when he's not on a massive world tour, which he announced earlier this week."

Love On Tour was set to kick off in April 2020 in Europe before sweeping through North America. But before it could even start, Harry was forced to postpone as the deadly COVID-19 virus spread across the globe. In his announcement, he urged fans to stay safe and self-isolate. "I can't wait to see you out on the road as soon as it's safe to do so. Until then, treat people with kindness." Harry followed his own advice, relaxing at home in Los Angeles with movie marathons, burritos, and face masks. Six weeks into the pandemic, with no end in sight, he switched gears: writing songs that would become his next album. And due to the lockdown, he did it all on his own without his go-to team. By the time Love On Tour finally kicked off seventeen months later in September 2021, he had already recorded his third album, *Harry's House*—except fans didn't know it yet.

In a time of uncertainty, he had found a silver lining. "It's been a pause that I don't know if I would have otherwise taken," Harry admitted to *Variety* in 2020. "I think it's been pretty good for me to have a kind of stop, to look and think about what it actually means to be an artist, what it means to do what we do and why we do it." Looking back, he realized it was fate that he reached peak creativity during a forced downtime. "If you asked anyone if they could go back to when they felt the best about making music, would they have made another album or done another tour? And I feel like everyone would take another album . . . in the moment where they feel like 'I can make stuff freely and feel really good about what I'm making,'" he explained to Apple Music's Zane Lowe.

Harry's House was released in May 2022 on the heels of his headlining performance at the Coachella Valley Music and Arts Festival. The first single, "As It Was," a synth-pop track about the singer losing and finding himself, entered the charts at No. 1, becoming his biggest hit to date complete with its own viral TikTok dance craze. "His full commercial potential has been unlocked, and now, everyone is demanding more of what he's selling," proclaimed *Billboard*. *Rolling Stone* deemed Harry "The World's Most Wanted Man." The singer even landed on the cover of *Better Homes & Gardens* for its 100th anniversary.

In 2023, as Love On Tour arrived on its fifth continent, Harry received arguably one of the most significant honors: *Harry's House* won Album of the Year at the *Grammys*, beating out Beyoncé, Adele, Coldplay,

"He does what feels right to him—and it seems to be universally appreciated."

Kendrick Lamar, Bad Bunny, Brandi Carlile, Lizzo, Mary J. Blige, and Abba. Superfans of each of the nominees were invited to stand onstage for the winner's announcement, and seventy-eight-year-old Styler, Reina Lafantaisie, got to do the honors. Harry ran right into her arms, embracing the Grammy Granny in a long hug.

His speech highlighted his admiration for the other artists in the category, all of whom had inspired him at some point. "I think on nights like tonight it's obviously so important for us to remember there is no such thing as 'best' in music," said Harry. "I'm so, so grateful . . . This doesn't happen to people like me very often."

For all the accolades, No. 1 albums, and sold-out concerts, Harry simply wants to enjoy making music "that I can be proud of for a long time," he revealed to *Better Homes & Gardens*. "That my friends can be proud of, that my family can be proud of, and that my kids will be proud of one day." Harry's mother, Anne Twist, credits his authenticity as the key to his phenomenal success. "He takes his influences from what he feels, what he's listened to, what he likes," she told the *Daily Mail* in 2023. "He does what feels right to him—and it seems to be universally appreciated."

KING OF KINGS

A modern-day Elvis Presley, Harry wanted nothing more than to portray The King in 2022's *Elvis*—but alas, his mega-fame proved to be a disadvantage. In 2019, Baz Luhrmann's long-simmering biopic was revived with the casting of Tom Hanks as Presley's controversial manager Colonel Tom Parker. Now all the film needed was its star. Harry, who had impressed with his debut in Christopher Nolan's *Dunkirk*, was one of the Hollywood up-and-comers vying for the role, including Miles Teller, Ansel Elgort, Aaron Taylor-Johnson, and Austin Butler. This would not have been the first time Harry slipped on The King's iconic white suit: as a kid, he impersonated Elvis in a school play—and he sent Luhrmann a video clip to convince the director to cast him. But ultimately, it was Harry's world-renowned face that swayed Luhrmann in the other direction.

"Harry is a really talented actor. I would work on something with him, [but] the real issue with Harry is, he's Harry Styles," he said on the *Fitzy and Wippa with Kate Ritchie* podcast. "He's already an icon." The other issue, added the Australian director, was that *Elvis* was set to begin production in January 2020, and it would last for eighteen months—but Harry had already committed to Love On Tour, which was scheduled to run at that time. *Elvis* went on to cast Butler, who earned an Academy Award nomination for Best Actor. Although it didn't work out with Harry, Luhrmann hopes they can work together in the future. "He is going to be a great actor, and he's already an iconic musician," the director gushed to *Entertainment Weekly*. "He is next level musically, and in terms of fashion, he's almost like Elvis himself . . . He's got the fluidity, visual thing. His music is always a surprise. He can be deep and meaningful. He can be light and poppy. He's just got it all. And he moves on stage. He's in the tradition of Elvis."

PART TWO

Music of the Times

DISCOGRAPHY

As a solo artist, the reformed pop star has leaned into his classic rock roots to create a twenty-first-century sound that's all his own. With each of his three albums, Harry has pushed the boundaries of his songwriting and artistry, often wearing his heart on his fashionable sleeve as he examines love in all its forms. His musical style has also matured as a pop rock blend that has dived deeper into its nostalgia: disco, funk, psychedelic, new wave, and even 1970s Japanese "city pop."

HARRY STYLES

THE POP STAR'S READY TO ROCK

RELEASE DATE: MAY 12, 2017

• TRACK LIST •

1. Meet Me in the Hallway
2. Sign of the Times
3. Carolina
4. Two Ghosts
5. Sweet Creature
6. Only Angel
7. Kiwi
8. Ever Since New York
9. Woman
10. From the Dining Table

CREATIVE DIRECTION: Although the album is self-titled, Harry shifts its lyrical focus to the women who have touched his life. "The one subject that hits the hardest is love, whether it's platonic, romantic, loving it, gaining it, losing it," he explained to *Rolling Stone* in 2017. "I don't think people want to hear me talk about going to bars, and how great everything is. The champagne popping . . . who wants to hear about it? I don't want to hear my favorite artists talk about all the amazing shit they get to do. I want to hear, 'How did you feel when you were alone in that hotel room because you chose to be alone?'" And the mood was set with a throwback sound that makes him sound especially emotional: classic rock. As the music of the 1960s and '70s is especially influential to the young singer. Indeed, Harry merged the past and present in the psychedelic, Pink Floyd–esque "Meet

Me in the Hallway" and soft rock "Two Ghosts" which reminded critics of George Harrison's solo work after the Beatles.

MAN BAND: His debut solo album was also Harry's first time working in the studio with musicians, his engineer-bassist Ryan Nasci, and guitarist Mitch Rowland (who went on to join his touring band). As for Harry, he played some guitar as well as the Omnichord, an electronic instrument that creates sounds using a Sonic Strings touchplate. "I'm happy I found this band and these musicians, where you can be vulnerable enough to put yourself out there," he told *Rolling Stone*. "I'm still learning . . . but it's my favorite lesson."

MUSICAL MESSAGE: The lead single, "Sign of the Times," started out as a seven-minute voice note on Harry's phone, a stream of consciousness in reaction to the 2016 political landscape when Donald Trump was elected president. Inspired by "the stuff that hurts me," such as people losing fundamentals like equal rights, Harry realized it wasn't the first time the world had endured adversity—and probably wouldn't be the last. "The song is written from a point of view as if a mother was giving birth to a child and there's a complication," he explained to *Rolling Stone*. "The mother is told, 'The child is fine, but you're not going to make it.' The mother has five minutes to tell the child, 'Go forth and conquer.'"

In the studio, the song came together quickly. Harry began tinkering around on the piano, then hopped onto the mic, "and we cut that whole record in three hours," producer Jeff Bhasker recalled to *Hits*. "And it sounded exactly like that: an instant classic-sounding record from conception to completion." Harry loved the meaning of "Sign of the Times" so much, he wanted to use it as the title of his album, but Bhasker suggested against it as Prince already did for his 1987 album, *Sign o' the Times*.

WHO'S THE MUSE?: Three years after Taylor Swift's Harry-heavy *1989*, he told his side of the story on his solo debut. The most obvious song is "Two Ghosts," which sounds like a direct lyrical response to Taylor's "Style." On the 2014 hit, she sings about her classic red lipstick and her man looking like 1950s actor James Dean in a white T-shirt. Harry's breakup ballad, coincidentally or not, is also about a couple with a girl who matches Taylor's description, except the guy has a couple more tattoos. When asked by BBC Radio 1's Nick Grimshaw, he couldn't deny the correlations. "I think it's pretty self-explanatory, right?" he replied with a laugh. Without naming names, Harry went on to explain the reasoning for his rhyme. "I think it's about, sometimes things change, and you can do all the same things, and sometimes it's just different, you know?"

The very pretty face who drove Harry crazy in the sexually charged "Kiwi" is not as unmistakable. Some fans theorized "Kiwi" was a nickname for Kendall Jenner, who was linked to the singer sporadically from 2013 to 2016. Although Harry admitted the reality star is "a huge part of the album," he wouldn't confirm which songs specifically. The most likely hint: "Kiwi" is a nickname for a New Zealander—the nationality of model Georgia Fowler, Harry's ex whom he dated in 2015.

The most obvious muse was someone never publicly connected to Harry: "Carolina" is about South Carolina native, Townes Adair Jones, who enjoyed one blind date with Harry in 2016. At the time, he was nearly done recording his album, yet in need of "a little bit of fun" on the track list. In the studio, he came up with a ditty based around the conversation

he'd had with Townes, about moving to Los Angeles for college on her grandmother's advice. Harry even name-dropped his date in the lyrics, but to unsuspecting fans the person remained a mystery.

CHART ATTACK: In the US, *Harry Styles* opened at No. 1 on the *Billboard* 200 with 230,000 album-equivalent units—the highest first sales week for a British male artist's debut (since Nielsen SoundScan first began tracking music sales in 1991). The lead single "Sign of the Times" also made history, reaching the top spot of the US iTunes chart in just nineteen minutes, shattering Adele's previous record of fifty minutes.

COVER STORY: Harry got everyone's attention when he dropped the cover art for his debut album: The singer is shirtless in pink-tinged water, bent over while holding his head in his hands. The focus of the photo is the lotus flower charm on his necklace, which was turned around so that it's seen hanging down his back. Literally dripping in symbolism, the lotus—an aquatic flower—references rebirth and overcoming adversity, which fans interpreted as the former boybander's statement on breaking free from One Direction. As for the color of the water, pink is the most popular shade for a lotus, but it was also the album's working title. "Pink is the only true rock & roll color," Harry told *Rolling Stone*, quoting the Clash bassist, Paul Simonon.

CARIBBEAN KINGS: After starting the recording process in Los Angeles, Harry felt the need to finish it in an unlikely place: Port Antonio, Jamaica, a remote region on the North Coast best known as the shipping point for coconuts and bananas. For two months in late 2016, the band lived and worked together at Geejam Studios, a compound previously utilized by the likes of Rihanna and Drake. Most mornings began with a swim in a nearby cove. To relax, Harry and guitarist Rowland binged rom-coms on Netflix, which inspired the spoken opening of Track 9, "Woman."

MAIN ATTRACTION: The solo artist's debut tour evolved along with his popularity. The first North American leg of Harry Styles: Live On Tour swept through smaller venues with just a few thousand in capacity—all dates sold out within seconds. By the European run in the spring of 2018, Harry's tour had quadrupled in size, and when he returned to the US that summer, he was playing in the country's biggest arenas, including back-to-back sold-out shows at Madison Square Garden in New York.

FINE LINE

HARRY CROSSES OVER INTO SUPERSTARDOM

RELEASE DATE: DECEMBER 13, 2019

• TRACK LIST •

1. Golden
2. Watermelon Sugar
3. Adore You
4. Lights Up
5. Cherry
6. Falling
7. To Be So Lonely
8. She
9. Sunflower, Vol. 6
10. Canyon Moon
11. Treat People with Kindness
12. Fine Line

HIGHS & LOWS: The themes of *Fine Line* range from happiness and sex to breakups and sadness. On the very first day of recording, Harry had to face the low end of the emotional spectrum when frequent collaborator Tom Hull (aka Kid Harpoon) walked into the studio wearing slippers he had received as a gift from Harry's ex-girlfriend Camille Rowe. "He looks at me and says, 'Where'd you get those slippers? They're nice,'" Hull recalled to *Rolling Stone*. "I had to say, 'Oh, um, your ex-girlfriend got them for me.' He said, '*Whaaaat?* How could you wear those?' He had a whole emotional journey about her, this whole relationship. But I kept saying, 'The best way of dealing with it is to put it in these songs you're writing.'"

CROSSING THE LINE: The title of the album hints at the boundary for Harry between his private personal life and what he reveals in his lyrics. As he explained to *Rolling Stone*, "It's not like I've ever sat and done an interview and said, 'So I was in a relationship, and this is what happened.' Because, for me, music is where I let that cross over. It's the *only* place, strangely, where it feels right to let that cross over."

FINE ART: The album's title takes on a different meaning in its cover image. Shot by Tim Walker in his signature fish-eye lens, the portrait depicts the *Fine Line* between masculinity and femininity, with Harry dressed in a fuchsia silk blouse and white wide-legged trousers. But it's the inside art that raised eyebrows—particularly, a nude photo of Harry lying near a severed heart with his hands artfully placed in his lap. "I'd never really done a shoot like this," he confessed on *The Ellen DeGeneres Show*. Walker, one of Harry's favorite photographers, didn't care for some of his subject's wardrobe choices. "It was like, 'This shirt's not really working so let's try it without the shirt.' And then it was, 'Those trousers aren't really working so let's try it without the trousers.' And then he looked at me and I was like, 'These pants aren't really working, are they?' So that was how it worked out . . . and now I'm naked."

HEARTBROKEN HARRY: Heading into the studio for his second solo album, he felt the pressure to match the success of *Harry Styles*. But it was producer Tyler Johnson who advised him to just "make the record that you want to make right now." However, at that moment, Harry was admittedly "not great" in the wake of his split from model Camille Rowe after a year of dating. Nursing a broken heart, he stayed up late one night and wrote "Cherry"—a mashup of their names—about his ex moving on with a new boyfriend, and how he'll miss her accent and friends. The recorded version includes Camille's voice, speaking in her native French, to a friend on the phone about their "perfect" day at the beach, which Harry captured while playing guitar at home. "She was actually speaking in the key of the song," he explained to *Rolling Stone*.

Camille also inspired "Falling," *Fine Line*'s third single. It only took Harry twenty minutes to knock out the ballad chronicling his emotional seesaw between feeling the happiest and saddest in his life. "The chorus says, 'What am I now? Am I someone I don't want around?' It was a big moment where I was asking myself, 'Who am I? What am I doing?'" Harry explained on Apple Music 1.

HIGH SPIRITS: During the recording process at the famed Shangri-La studio in Malibu, Harry experimented with psychedelics and chocolate edibles to expand his creative mind. "We'd do mushrooms, lie down on the grass, and listen to Paul McCartney's *Ram* in the sunshine," he revealed to *Rolling Stone*. "We'd just turn the speakers into the yard." One night while high, he inexplicably jumped out the window. When he landed, his chin hit his knee—and bit off the end of his tongue. "It was bleeding quite heavily," he recalled on *The Howard Stern Show*. "It was pretty painful." Another time, while partying on the beach with his band, Harry somehow lost all his clothes. "Maybe a month later, somebody found my wallet and mailed it back, anonymously. I guess it just popped out of the sand. But what's sad is, I lost my favorite mustard corduroy flares."

PARADISE FOUND?: Just before Harry announced his second single, "Adore You," a mysterious island with a similar name popped up on social media. Ads targeted at fans promoted the Isle of Eroda ("Adore" spelled backward), a tropical paradise where residents wearing bold hairstyles live in quaint villages with pubs and bakeries known for delectable pastries—all nods at the former One Direction member. The official website, VisitEroda.com, went even more in-depth, with recommendations on where to stay (Seaview Cottages), where to drink (Sally's Tavern), and where to indulge (Adoré Salon and Spa). There were even testimonials from visitors and locals all praising Eroda's natural beauty, cuisine, and vivacious art scene.

Stylers believed Eroda was connected to Harry, then put the dots together as they learned more about *Fine Line*. One tourist commented on Twitter (now known as X) that they couldn't wait to return on December 13, the same day as the album's release. There were also hints in the track list: The Fisherman's Pub is located at the corner of Cherry Street and Golden Way, each road named after a song; Eroda is known for its juicy watermelons—wink, wink, "Watermelon Sugar." Alas, it was too good to be true: Eroda was a fantasy land invented to promote "Adore You."

Harry gave fans a visual of the paradise in the single's eight-minute video, which explores Eroda and its folklore. Narrated by Spanish singer Rosalía, "Adore You" follows Harry's character, The Boy, a lonely local who rescues a dying jewel-coat fish he finds on the shore. He adores his new pet, singing to it and taking it sightseeing around the seaside town. But as the fish grows, The Boy must scour Eroda for bigger water tanks—and in the process, reveals glimpses of the island's make-believe Adoré Salon, Seaview Cottage, and Flanagan Fish Market.

KID-FRIENDLY: The fourth single, "Watermelon Sugar," was the sleeper hit of *Fine Line*, reaching the Top 10 in more than twenty countries, and earning Harry his first Grammy in 2021 for Best Pop Solo Performance. Why was it so universally appealing? "I've never had a song connect with children in this way," Hull explained to *Variety*. "I get sent videos all the time from friends of their kids singing. I have a three-year-old and an eight-year-old, and they listen to it." The pop-funk song's success is somewhat perplexing to Harry, who almost cut it from the album. Early in the production process, he liked "Watermelon Sugar," but "then I kind of really hated it for a long time," he confessed during his NPR Tiny Desk Concert performance. "It kept kind of coming back into the mix."

BREAKING RECORDS: *Fine Line*, Harry's second consecutive album to debut at No. 1 on the *Billboard* 200 chart, sold 478,000 album-equivalent units in its first week, setting the record for the biggest debut from a British male artist since Nielsen SoundScan began in 1991.

HARRY'S HOUSE

THE FOUNDATION OF HIS BEST SONGWRITING

RELEASE DATE: MAY 20, 2022

• TRACK LIST •

1. Music for a Sushi Restaurant
2. Late Night Talking
3. Grapejuice
4. As It Was
5. Daylight
6. Little Freak
7. Matilda
8. Cinema
9. Daydreaming
10. Keep Driving
11. Satellite
12. Boyfriends
13. Love of My Life

EASTERN INFLUENCE: For his third album, Harry expanded his scope of the rock genre. After spending a good chunk of 2019 in Tokyo, he brought back a musical souvenir: city pop, a blend of various genres including disco, R&B, and funk that was popular in Japan in the 1970s and '80s. During the making of *Harry's House*, he also made a conscious effort not to listen to traditional pop, gravitating more towards jazz and instrumental, which inspired him to focus on conveying emotion through music rather than lyrics. The godfather of Japanese pop, Haruomi Hosono, had a major influence on the album as well. While in Tokyo, Harry heard his 1973 folk-rock album *Hosono House* and thought "Oh, I love that." More so, he was intrigued by how Hosono made it: every afternoon, he spent five hours recording in his bedroom with a sixteen-track mixing console in his living room.

Borrowing this concept, Harry intended to make music outside of a studio. For the most part, he did. Some songs were tracked at a friend's house, although Harry and his band did eventually book time at the famed Shangri-La studio in Malibu, originally a two-acre ranch with a bungalow in the late 1950s.

But instead of recording in the control room, they moved all equipment into one room. "When I took that title [*Harry's House*] and put it to the songs we were making, it felt like it took on this whole new meaning. It was about: 'Okay, imagine it's a day in my house—what do I go through? A day in my mind—what do I go through?' In my house, I'm playing fun music, I'm playing sad music," he mused to Zane Lowe during an eighty-minute in-depth conversation they had on a poolside in Palm Springs, California. The way he imagined it, "I'm going to play in my house, and you can come visit 100 percent, [but] I'm making this because it's what I want to listen to. This is like my favorite album at the moment. I love it so much."

FAITHFUL FANS: A full month before the official release of *Harry's House*, the album leaked onto several social media platforms. "PSA: friends don't let friends listen to *Harry's House* before May 20," tweeted Sony Music. Loyal fans resisted the temptation—and implored casuals to do the same. On Reddit, the Harry Styles community page laid out a bulleted list of its stance: sharing the link to listen (or even asking for it) would bring on banishment, and any discussion about the leaked tracks was prohibited.

On Twitter (now known as X), fans vowed to block any users who promoted the unauthorized version of the album. However, it was quite the opposite on TikTok, where a song called "Baby Honey" that is not on the final *Harry's House* track list popped up in thousands of user-generated videos.

AS IT ALMOST WASN'T: The lead single off *Harry's House* topped the charts in forty-five countries, but "As It Was" almost ended up on the cutting room floor. When Harry played some of the final songs for Sony Music CEO Rob Stringer, "I was like: 'I don't know if this'll be on the record or anything.' That kind of uncertainty is always the best." Fans certainly agreed: "As It Was" pulled in 180.9 million streams in 2022.

WHERE THE HEART IS: To the casual ear, "Love of My Life" sounded like an ode to someone who has Harry's heart. But a closer listen reveals he's not singing about a person, but a place: England. At the start of the 2020 COVID-19 lockdown, he found himself stranded in Los Angeles, five thousand miles (8,047 km) away from where he wanted to be. This inspired the final track on his album, which reminisces Sunday afternoon walks and good times at his friend Jonny's place, neither of which feel the same anymore. "I've always wanted to write a song about like home and loving England and all that kind of stuff. And it's always kinda hard to do without being like 'went to the chippy and I did this thing,'" Harry explained to Zane Lowe on Apple Music 1.

"Love of My Life" is the spirit of *Harry's House*, he explains, because of its sparse acoustic sound, the original feeling for his third album—which he had hoped to literally record at his home. But it was the figurative sense that convinced him otherwise. "It took time for me to realize that the house

wasn't a geographical location, it was an internal thing," he told Lowe. "When I applied that concept to the songs we were making here, everything took on new meaning."

DEAR JOHN: One of the most esteemed musicians in modern times lent his five-string talents to *Harry's House*. John Mayer played electric guitar on two tracks, "Cinema" and "Daydreaming," adding a funk groove to both. The two singers have been tight for some time. Back in 2011, Harry tweeted about reuniting with John, "Oh how I've missed you." Two years later, John photographed Harry in Tokyo for a black-and-white portrait series. Fans hoped he would make an appearance on Love On Tour—and he did, just in the audience and not onstage. At Harry's Los Angeles concert in October 2022, the "Gravity" singer was spotted dancing along to "As It Was."

Harry and John share a very specific commonality: they both dated Taylor Swift and inspired her to write songs about their relationships. And fans spotted what seemed like Harry's own Easter egg on *Harry's House*: "Cinema" and "Daydreaming" are Tracks 8 and 9 . . . and Taylor's *1989* album features at least seven songs written about her time with the One Direction heartthrob.

CHASING DAYLIGHT: Harry and his producers, Kid Harpoon and Tyler Johnson, literally did not "sleep till the daylight" when recording the album's fifth track. The trio tinkered with the psychedelic-pop song well into the early morning hours, but Harry refused to call it a night. "We have to find a way to stay awake and finish this because if we all go to bed, then this [isn't] gonna turn out [the way we want it to]," he recalled telling Harpoon and Johnson, who played all the instruments on the track. They powered through—and celebrated by watching the sunrise on the beach in Malibu.

HEALING WORDS: When Harry played "Matilda" for several of his friends, there wasn't a dry eye in the house. The sentimental song was inspired by a female pal who nonchalantly revealed details about her childhood that made Harry think, "Oh that's not normal," he revealed on Apple Music 1. Unsure if it was his place to tell her so, Harry decided to write about what was weighing on his mind. Drawing comparisons to the Roald Dahl literary character Matilda, a brilliant little girl unloved by her parents, Harry encourages his friend to disengage from her family for her own peace. Harry never told "Matilda" about the song she inspired, but he assumed she would figure it out when she listened to the album.

Talking with Lowe about his past regrets for not helping friends who have struggled with mental health, he saw "Matilda" as a way to offer healing. "With something like this, it's kind of like, 'I want to give you something, I want to support you in some way,' but it's not necessarily my place to make it about me. Because it's not my experience . . . If nothing else, it just says, 'I was listening to you.'"

ALBUM OF THE YEAR: *Harry's House* was one of the highlights of 2022 and it was an immediate hit. Within two hours of its release, the album notched the most first-day streams on Apple Music for a pop album that year. In the UK, it was the fastest-selling album in 2022.

PART THREE

Very Harry

HARRY A TO Z

Our favorite singer is endlessly fascinating. Whether you consider yourself a Styler, a member of The Harries, or a Day One Directioner, there are always new things to learn about Harry Styles: the book that changed his life, the hobby he picked up during COVID-19 lockdown, the unlikely exercise that's kept him in shape over the past decade. These are the essential fun facts all fans should know, from the animal lover's special bond with dogs to Ziggy Stardust, David Bowie's 1970s alter ego who influenced the millennial's modern glam-rock style.

ANIMAL LOVER

Harry has a soft spot for all creatures big and small: turtles (his favorite), dogs, cats, rabbits, hamsters, even pigeons. From the time he was a baby, he's loved dogs—and the feeling is mutual. The family pet, a Border collie–lurcher mix named Max, would often lie on the floor with the toddler or hop in his crib. Once, remembered his older sister, Gemma, Harry spat out his pacifier and put it in the dog's mouth "like something out of *The Simpsons*. Max looked somewhat puzzled but just sort of let him get on with it. Harry has that way about him." And not much has changed over the years. Social media is filled with fan photos of Harry posing with random pups he's met in public—and one in particular has an amusing story behind it.

In 2018, the singer was standing outside the Oaks Gourmet Market & Cafe in Hollywood when he noticed a man with a dog who couldn't enter the restaurant to pick up his food because of a strict no-pet policy. "Harry Styles saw my predicament, tapped me on the shoulder, and said he could watch Oscar while I went in," Rory Carroll tweeted, along with a photo of the superstar holding his six-month-old Labrador's leash—which of course went viral. Carroll was interviewed by *Good Morning America* and revealed that Harry took the responsibility seriously. "I could see him through the large restaurant windows while I was inside and he kept his eyes focused on Oscar the whole time, never looking at his phone." The situation was so unbelievable that Carroll asked Harry if he could take a photo for proof, and "he happily obliged."

Early on in his career, Harry got involved with The Dolphin Project, a nonprofit that raises awareness about the cruelty of dolphin captivity. While in San Diego for a One Direction concert in 2013, he asked fans if they liked dolphins, and when they applauded, he urged them, "Don't go to SeaWorld." The theme park management knew the power of Harry's words and immediately put out a statement insisting that they "love dolphins too" and that they "care for the animals" in their parks "like we would our own family."

Harry's love for animals even inspired his diet. In 2017, he became a pescatarian, meaning he abstains from meat but eats fish. "My body definitely feels better for it," he told *Vogue*, explaining that he was inspired to make the change by several band members who were vegan.

BEACHWOOD CAFE

In "Falling," Harry reminisces on his relationship with Camille Rowe, particularly their go-to breakfast spot, the Beachwood Cafe. Located in the Hollywood Hills enclave of Beachwood Canyon, the restaurant has been a local favorite for decades—and thanks to Stylers, it found new prominence after 2019's *Fine Line*. Fans regularly stop by the Beachwood Cafe to check out the buzzed-about coffee and Harry's favorite Beachwood Scramble, and if they're lucky, they might get the chance to sit in his corner booth. But during Harry's three-night stand at Kia Forum in January 2023, hundreds took over the mom-and-pop joint, lining up down the block in the canyon's town square even before 8 a.m.

Beachwood Cafe wholeheartedly embraces its famous connection to Harry: "Falling" plays as its phone line's hold music; "The Coffee's Out" mugs, T-shirts, and hats have been added to the restaurant's merchandise collection; even the tip jar on the counter references Harry—even though he hasn't been seen in Beachwood Canyon since his 2018 split from Camille.

Set in a circus, the singer juggles, walks a tightrope, and is shot out of a canon wearing a pair of wings so he can "fly to you."

CAR COLLECTION

Harry is a man with varied tastes in music, fashion, women, and cars. His fleet ranges from practical and exotic to vintage and is worth millions. The singer's first set of wheels was a 1973 Ford Capri that he reportedly paid $10,000 for not long after turning eighteen. For his nineteenth birthday, Harry gifted himself a brand-new red Porsche Cayman S with a $65,000 sticker price and the capability to go from zero to sixty in 4.7 seconds. Around this time, he picked up a second sports car, a 2012 silver Audi R8 Coupe that cost a whopping $120,000.

There are several vintage cars in Harry's collection, with the oldest being a 1966 Mercedes-Benz 230SL convertible that he was spotted driving in 2014 around West Hollywood. The most exotic is arguably a yellow 1972 Ferrari Dino 246 GT estimated to be worth $362,000. Harry loves the Jaguar E-Type Roadster so much that he has two: a 1971 red convertible—valued at $465,000—that he keeps in London and a 1972 silver hardtop version that doesn't have a working radio for tooling around Los Angeles. Similarly, Harry has a pair of midsize SUVs in each of the two cities where he spends most of his free time: a Range Rover and an electric Tesla Model X.

DAYLIGHT VIDEO (UNOFFICIAL)

Although "Daylight" from *Harry's House* was never an official single, the track has not one, but two music videos. The first visual is actually the unofficial version—made in just three hours for only $300. In May 2022, James Corden enlisted the singer for a segment on *The Late Late Show* that found the pair knocking on apartment doors in New York City, looking to convince someone to open up their home for the video shoot. After several failed attempts, they finally struck gold with four young women who just so happened to be fans of Harry Styles. A few excited phone calls later and they had enough extras to create a party scene for "Daylight," which follows the singer as he wanders through the apartment completely ignored by revelers.

Another sequence is a literal take on the song's opening line as Harry dances atop the Brooklyn building at sunset, dressed like a clown in a gold sequined bowler hat and oversized red bow tie that he had found downstairs in a closet. Despite being Corden's directorial debut—and made on a shoestring budget—the charming video was masterful and surpassed ten million views on YouTube.

Over a year later, Harry surprised fans when he released an official "Daylight" video with a similar theme. Set in a circus, the singer juggles, walks a tightrope, and is shot out of a canon wearing a pair of wings so he can "fly to you."

ERSKINE RECORDS

When Harry signed with Columbia Records in 2016, he did so in partnership with his own independent label, Erskine Records. The deal allows the artist to own the copyright of his music catalog while Columbia holds a license agreement on each of the albums. Harry was the codirector of the company, along with his personal assistant Emma Spring. It is believed to be named after Erskine House, the historic North London residence he purchased in 2012 as One Direction was just taking off. According to financial statements filed in September 2023, Erskine Records owned £63.6 million ($80.4 million) in assets.

That year, Harry signed his first artist: Mitch Rowland, the guitarist from his band. During the pandemic, Rowland wrote his album, *Come June*, and when his original record deal ultimately fell through, Harry's manager Jeffrey Azoff suggested he put it out with Erskine. Harry was also a sounding board for Rowland early in the process.

When he was unsure of a song called "Here Comes the Comeback," he sent it to the singer for feedback. "Immediately, he loved it," Rowland told *NME*. "Every time I saw him, he'd be playing it off his phone, so I thought, 'Hm, maybe there's something in it'. Eventually, we were making part of *Harry's House* and he's like, 'Can I have it?' So, I did hear him sing on it and it stayed like that for a while, then he put it on the shelf, and no one talked about it so I asked for it back." For several 2023 dates on Harry's Love On Tour, Rowland pulled double duty, opening for the headliner as well as playing guitar in his band.

FAVORITE BOOK

As a kid, Harry wasn't much of a bookworm, but he's grown into quite a voracious reader now. "I had such a short attention span," he explained to *Rolling Stone* in 2019. "But I was dating someone who gave me some books; I felt like I had to read them because she'd think I was a dummy if I didn't read them." Ever since then, he's collected an impressive library spanning historical romance novels, feminist literature, celebrity memoirs, and thirteenth-century poetry.

One of his favorite authors is Haruki Murakami, a Japanese novelist whose works have been translated into fifty languages. Harry's creative director Molly Hawkins gave him a copy of Murakami's *Norwegian Wood*, a nostalgic tale of a man reminiscing on 1960s Tokyo after hearing the Beatles' song of the same name. "It was the first book, maybe ever, where all I wanted to do all day was read this," revealed Harry. "I think every man should read *Norwegian Wood*," added Hawkins. "Harry's the only man I've given it to who actually read it."

Three books have literally changed his life. *Siddhartha*, Hermann Hesse's 1922 novel about a man's spiritual journey of self-discovery, "makes a lot of sense to me" and especially resonated with him while he was traveling with a friend. In 2015, Harry was photographed carrying a copy of one of his two favorite books of all time, Rumi's *Selected Poems*, which explores love and devotion through vivid imagery of nature. His third pick is Charles Bukowski's most popular collection of poetry, *Love Is a Dog from Hell*. "I just love the way [he] uses language," Harry told *Another Man* magazine. "It's so real, gritty, and filthy, yet there is something so romantic about it."

A fan of classic rock, Harry's done his homework and studied his heroes: He's read *Life* by Rolling Stones guitarist Keith Richards and Elton John's *Me*. Another book from the same late-1960s era, Richard Brautigan's *In Watermelon Sugar*, inspired his 2019 hit. While in the studio working on his second album, he was struggling to come up with lyrics for the chorus. On a table was Richard Brautigan's post-apocalyptic novel set in an idyllic commune called iDEATH. The plot has nothing to do with Harry's song, but the book's title did cure his writer's block. "I was like, 'That would sound cool.'"

GREEN BAY PACKERS

Growing up near Manchester, Harry is, of course, a fan of the soccer club Manchester United, who have won a record twenty titles in the Premier League. But when he first visited America in 2012, he got into the country's most popular sport, football—particularly the Green Bay Packers, who have the most wins from any National Football League (NFL) franchise. Harry's so obsessed with the team that he owns Packers shirts, jerseys, hats, helmets, a blanket, and even an apron. Of the sixty-plus tattoos on his body, the team's logo is etched onto his bicep!

It seems pretty random for a Brit to be a superfan of a sports team from "America's Dairyland." Harry explained how he became a "cheesehead" (the nickname for Packers enthusiasts) in an interview with NPR, decked out in an Aaron Rodgers jersey no less. "When I first started traveling to Los Angeles, I would stay with a friend who is from Appleton, Wisconsin, so those were the first games that I watched. And we used to play [the video game] Madden, but I was always playing as the Green Bay

Packers. They're also the only NFL team owned by the fans, you know I like that . . . also a big fan of cheese, so yeah, Packers were the team for me."

The team is so immensely popular, that home games at Lambeau Field have been sold out since 1960—and the waiting list for tickets is at least 147,000 names long! Harry lucked out in 2014 when he got the opportunity to witness the Packers defeat the Kansas City Chiefs in Wisconsin. "It was great," he recounted in 2020. "It was a preseason game, and I was told the atmosphere was like the playoffs everywhere else."

HARRYWEEN

Harry loves to dress up 365 days a year, but on October 31, he really gets into the holiday spirit. In 2021, he kicked off the two-night Harryween, a Halloween-themed concert, at Madison Square Garden in New York. The singer strongly encouraged fans to dress accordingly—and he led the costume parade. The first night, he stepped onstage as Dorothy from *The Wizard of Oz*, complete with a blue gingham dress, Toto in a picnic basket, and ruby slippers (which he clicked, much to the delight of the crowd). Harry's band rounded out the film's cast of characters: Tin Man, Scarecrow, the Cowardly Lion, the Wicked Witch, Glinda the Good Witch, and the Wizard. For the second night, he dressed as the seventeenth-century "sad clown" Pierrot, but with a haute-couture twist: a white-ruffled Gucci suit. Fans didn't disappoint, either: the arena was packed with superheroes, angels, cheerleaders, flappers, unicorns, and even a pair of zombies with a sign reading "Eat People with Kindness," a post-apocalyptic take on Harry's motto to "Treat People with Kindness."

Harryween was so spooktacular that he hosted the second annual event, this time for West Coast fans, at the Kia Forum in Los Angeles. Once

"They're also the only NFL team owned by the fans . . . also a big fan of cheese, so yeah, Packers were the team for me."

again, Harry masqueraded as a cinematic icon: *Grease*'s Danny Zuko, made famous by John Travolta. Decked out in a black leather jacket bedazzled with "Harryween" on the back, the singer walked onstage to "You're the One That I Want," with his band of Greasers and Pink Ladies. Harry also paid tribute to *Grease*'s Sandy, the late Olivia Newton-John, with a cover of "Hopelessly Devoted to You."

Fans held out hope for a 2023 Harryween, but it was all trick and no treat: after two years of nonstop touring, Harry took a well-deserved break.

ISOLATION AND SELF-IMPROVEMENT

In March 2020, Harry was set to return home to England to spend time with family before heading out on Love On Tour while the world had other

plans. As the COVID-19 virus forced billions into lockdown, air travel was grounded—leaving Harry "stuck" in Los Angeles. But he made the most of his time in isolation, focusing on mental health and exercise, writing new music, practicing guitar, reading, watching movies, and "doing some face masks." He even picked up a few new hobbies to better himself: The Gucci brand ambassador learned to speak Italian and took sign language classes. Two years later, he showed off his new skills when a fan threw a chicken nugget onstage at New York's Madison Square Garden. As the crowd cheered, "Eat it! Eat it!" the pescatarian replied, "Sorry, I don't eat meat. Non mangi carne."

During his time in quarantine, Harry tried to maintain a routine amid the chaos around the world. "I'll meditate in the morning, and then have a coffee and do some reading to kind of just try to wake up a little bit," he told Zane Lowe in a FaceTime virtual interview on Apple Music 1. "And then I go for a run, try and get some air and some sunshine, and try and work out in the morning or something. And then I'll try to do a little work and just go for a walk in the afternoon. I have just been trying to get some air and not see anyone. But I've been going for drives and stuff just to get some air and some sun on my face."

Like so many other artists, he used the time to create music— "As It Was" from 2022's *Harry's House* reflects on the loneliness of isolation. During lockdown, he predicted "a lot of powerful music is going to come from [this] because ultimately you have people who have a need to express themselves through music and writing and film and so many different ways, who are now having a lot of extra time with no distractions." Harry was right: not only did Taylor Swift release two albums' worth of material (*folklore* and *evermore*) in 2020, but Beyoncé also conceived and recorded *Renaissance* as a way of sparking "joy" for fans coming out of the global pandemic.

"I'm just a friend with him and there was never any 'flame.'"

JAPAN SOJOURN

After wrapping his first solo tour, Harry returned to Japan, "one of my favorite places," for a monthslong journey of self-discovery. Fans spotted him in December 2018 wandering around the streets of Tokyo like any other tourist. Days after the new year, the famous singer popped up at a local karaoke bar where he treated patrons to Nirvana's "Smells Like Teen Spirit" decked out in a pair of "2019" eyeglasses. During his time in the country, Harry got really into jazz music—and introduced a bartender at his favorite vinyl bar to Paul McCartney's band Wings by giving him a copy of their 1979 album *Back to the Egg*. "'Arrow Through Me,' that was the song I had to hear every day when I was in Japan," he told *Rolling Stone*. For Harry's twenty-fifth birthday that February, "I had grilled fish and miso soup for breakfast, then I went to this café. I sat and drank tea and read for five hours." His book of choice: Haruki Murakami's *The Wind-Up Bird Chronicle*, a psychological fiction novel about a man who searches for his wife's missing cat and ends up in a Tokyo underworld.

But he didn't spend the special day completely alone. That evening, Harry had dinner with friends, including rumored love interest Japanese American model, Kiko Mizuhara. The group then headed to a karaoke bar, where Harry led a sing-along of Queen's "Bohemian Rhapsody." Kiko, one of the most-followed people on Instagram in Japan, adamantly denied any romance with the handsome Brit at the time, although they clearly had a lasting connection. In March 2023, Harry was spotted with Kiko while in Tokyo for his Love On Tour. The two were caught by security cameras at 6 a.m. walking in the rain through the Kabukicho entertainment district—Harry wearing angel wings, Kiko in a pink wig—capping off a wild night out that included his public make-out session with model Emily Ratajkowski. "Harry came to a party I was hosting toward the very end," Kiko told the *Daily Mail*. "As the party ended in the morning, we went to have breakfast and I dropped him off on my way home. I'm just a friend with him and there was never any 'flame.'"

KNIT-TOK

While rehearsing for an outdoor concert on NBC's *Today* show in February 2020, Harry kept warm in a color-block patchwork cardigan that sparked a TikTok trend. Dubbed the #HarryStylesCardigan challenge, social media users were inspired to knit their own version of his JW Anderson sweater and share their progress on the platform. Within months, the hashtag had over forty-one million views! Jonathan Anderson was so appreciative of the viral marketing, the UK designer rolled up his sleeves to help them knock off the $1,560 garment: he released a downloadable detailed pattern for crochet enthusiasts to follow—and uploaded a step-by-step video tutorial by his Senior Knitwear Designer on YouTube (which has surpassed one million views).

The #HarryStylesCardigan challenge came at a pivotal time as the world went into lockdown to safeguard against COVID-19. Recognized as "an emblem of the DIY creativity" inspired by that time, Harry's knitwear was added to the permanent collection of London's Victoria and Albert Museum where five centuries of fashion are on display. "I am so impressed and incredibly humbled by the whole thing," Anderson gushed in a statement. "It's been incredible to see everyone knitting the cardigan on their own and with the pattern we released and to see so many people making it their own. Donating the cardigan to the V&A feels like the right next step to acknowledge everyone's incredible creativity and craft, especially during such a challenging time in history."

LOVE ON TOUR

Quite literally, Harry brought love to the world with Love On Tour—several fans were inspired to get engaged mid-concert. In Lisbon, in August 2022, a young man named Carl caught Harry's eye with a sign that read "Help me propose." But that wasn't all. "Can I sing two lines to my girlfriend?" he asked. Harry obliged and handed over the microphone—and then stood there flabbergasted as Carl flawlessly crooned Elvis Presley's "Can't Help Falling in Love" to his shocked girlfriend, Mariana. Harry watched adoringly on the Jumbotron as the fan got down on one knee.

Six months later in Brisbane, Australia, a female fan named Connie took a different approach with her sign: "Make my boyfriend propose." "First of all, 'make' is aggressive," joked Harry. "Ask?" After making sure her boyfriend, Stevan, was game, Harry passed him a microphone and he said, "I just want to say how good Harry Styles is, but there's somebody I love more. Will you marry me?"

In March 2023, just days later in Singapore, Harry requested his band play "some romantic music" as another fan got down on one knee. "She said yes!" Harry announced to the cheering crowd. "Kenneth and Kimmy, everybody . . . You both seem wonderful. I wish you a life of happiness."

MENTAL HEALTH ADVOCATE

As Harry stepped into his solo career, he couldn't shake some of the anxieties ingrained in him as a former member of One Direction. The pressure of being in the world's most popular boy band manifested in different ways. During live performances, he was "constantly scared" he would sing the wrong notes. Offstage, he felt he always had to be overly polite for fear someone might tell the press he was rude. Then there was what he called "emotionally coasting" through 1D's meteoric success. "We'd go through real highs in the band and stuff, and it would always just feel like a relief. Like, 'Oh, we didn't fail. That feels like a massive relief,'" he explained in a 2019 radio interview on Apple Music 1. "I never really felt like I celebrated anything." In the years after the group split, Harry tried to work through some of the issues on his own, but it "got to a point when I realized I was in my own way." Living in California, it seems like everyone was in therapy, "and I think for a long time I was like, 'I don't need that.' You know, it's very like [a] British way of looking at it, I think."

Harry was ultimately convinced to talk to a professional after one friend described it to him as, "You can tell somebody everything. You can talk at somebody, pay them, and then they are not allowed to tell anyone."

The superstar found a trusted therapist in LA and whenever he was out of town, they would hold long-distance sessions over the phone. "I thought about getting one in London, but, for me, it is much easier to have one person who is a vessel, who I can tell everything to," he explained to Howard Stern in 2020. "If I started having two different people, it would confuse me a bit." Harry committed to his therapist once a week—and it had a profound impact on his life. "It's helped me just be more present," he told *Vogue*. "I feel like I'm able to enjoy the things that are happening right in front of me, even if it's food or it's coffee or it's being with a friend."

In November 2021, one of the seventeen thousand in attendance at Harry's Los Angeles concert was his therapist, who got a special shoutout from the stage. "There are some people in this room tonight who have helped me more than I could ever express to them, and you all know who you are," he said. "I just want to say thank you. Because you changed my life, and I'm so happy. This is a hundred percent my favorite thing to do, and I appreciate you being here tonight so much . . . In potentially the most LA thing that has ever come out of my mouth. My therapist is here. So thank you to her."

NET WORTH

The richest British celebrity under thirty in 2022 and 2023, Harry has an estimated net worth of £150 million ($190 million). During his five years in One Direction, he earned a reported $23 million. But once he broke out on his own, Harry's bank account inflated exponentially. His solo contract with Columbia paid out $80 million for three albums—but it's his two sold-out world tours that have doubled Harry's wealth. Live On Tour pulled in $63 million, making it one of the most popular shows of 2018.

"In potentially the most LA thing that has ever come out of my mouth: my therapist is here. So thank you to her."

Three years later, Love On Tour raked in a whopping ten times more: $617.3 million, setting the record for fourth highest-grossing tour of all time (Taylor Swift's The Eras Tour and Beyoncé's Renaissance World Tour ultimately pushed Harry down to sixth place).

The singer's burgeoning film career has also padded his net worth. He reportedly earned $3.4 million for his acting debut in *Dunkirk* and another $2.5 million for *Don't Worry Darling*. Harry turned his $380,000 *Eternals* cameo into a $100 million payday when he signed a deal with Marvel Studios in 2022 to reprise his character, Eros, in five additional films within the superhero cinematic universe.

In the world of fashion, Harry cashed in on being the muse of Gucci creative director Alessandro Michele. In 2019, British *Vogue* reported he earned £8 million ($10 million) as an ambassador for the Italian luxury label. The role entailed starring in several Gucci Men's Tailoring campaigns and exclusively wearing the brand on red carpets.

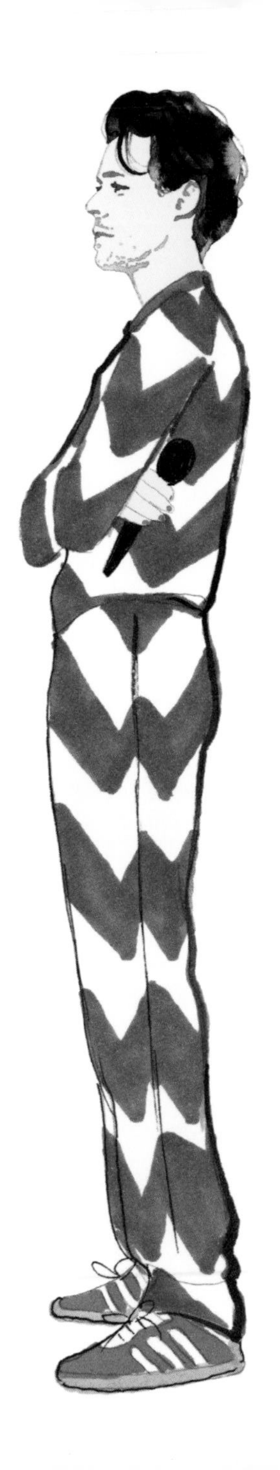

ONE DIRECTION REUNION

Ever since One Direction went on hiatus in 2015, fans have been holding out hope that the boy band would get back together. Four out of the five members have publicly stated that they're open to a reunion at some point, with Harry perhaps being the most supportive. "I love the band and would never rule out anything in the future," he told *Rolling Stone* in 2017. "The band changed my life, gave me everything." He expressed the same sentiment when the magazine asked him the question again in 2019. "If there's a time when we all really *want* to do it, that's the only time for us to do it . . . I think even in the disagreements, there's always a mutual respect for each other—we did this really cool thing together, and we'll always have that. It's too important to me to ever be like, 'Oh, that's done.' But if it happens, it will happen for the right reasons."

Liam Payne had a different reaction to the continual questioning. In 2019, a fan tweeted about conflicting statements he had made about a 1D reunion happening in 2020 to coincide with the tenth anniversary of the boy band's debut on *The X Factor*—and Liam was exasperated, to say the least. "Can people stop passing blame to me," he shot back on Twitter (now known as X). "I get asked this ridiculous question 500× a day (exaggeration)." But in all sincerity, Liam explained, the topic is brought up so often that his answers tend to vary. Still, that didn't stop him from stoking the flames months later with a loose timetable for 1D's reunion. "All I know is that there are at least two years because everyone's released new music and you have to go and promo," Liam explained on the UK talk show, *Sunday Brunch*. "There are at least two years."

Of the five, Louis Tomlinson took the split the hardest: "I was absolutely gutted," he told the *Times* in 2023. "I do miss the boys and I do definitely

"I was the one with the long hair.
I had it for so much
of One Direction . . . cutting it off
very much felt like starting it fresh."

miss being one of the five, but I like doing my own thing too." Although getting the band back together was "hard to imagine right now," Louis did say he would "be up for it." Niall Horan questioned what constituted a 1D reunion. "It could be like the *Friends* reunion," which was simply a TV special of the cast reminiscing. "It could be a whole tour," he mused to Zane Lowe in 2023. "God knows what it is, but no, it hasn't been spoken about."

PILATES

Harry's washboard abs and toned arms are the result of years of Pilates, a low-impact form of mind-body exercise that strengthens muscles and increases flexibility. He first got into it at eighteen years old in order to improve his posture and soon became a regular at Exhale Pilates London.

"With Pilates, Harry predominately works with core, breathing, and lung capacity—because of his singing—and with his hamstrings because he's moving all the time," his longtime instructor, Gaby Noble told the *Daily Mail*. "He's become much more nimble." During their one-on-one sessions, Harry works out using a variety of Pilates equipment including his two favorites: Reformer, a spring-based resistance machine, and Wunda Chair, which strengthens muscle groups not easily reached by traditional techniques.

In 2023, Exhale Pilates featured their most famous client in a "Men of Exhale" compilation video to squash the stigma that Pilates is just for women. In the split-second clip of Harry, the singer works on his core while holding a weighted bar over his head. It caused such a stir on Instagram that Noble was inspired to offer virtual classes through Exhale Pilates London so Stylers around the world can achieve the same mind-body benefits as their favorite singer.

QUIFF QUEST

Harry's floppy hair has been a *mane* attraction ever since his 1D days—and the obsession grew along with the length of his wavy locks. By 2015, his quiff (a British term for a high-styled bouffant) was down past his shoulders, a hint at the rock star he would become as a solo artist.

However, when the boy band went their separate ways, he chopped it all off and fans got to witness the moment in Apple Music's 2017 documentary, *Harry Styles: Behind the Album*. With his mother Anne standing by for support, the singer covered his face as the scissors sheared his long locks. "I was the one with the long hair. I had it for so much of One Direction . . . cutting it off very much felt like starting it fresh," he explained.

While on tour, Harry brought along a hairstylist to ensure his curly coiffure withstood the show's high energy demands. "He shakes his hair around while he's performing, so I have to think about that movement when I'm doing his hair," Ayae Yamamoto revealed to *People* magazine, detailing her process. "I really consider the location of the show and the current weather—the humidity makes a difference when it's an outdoor show. We start with wet hair, and I try to use drying products to counteract the movement and sweat . . . I want to have it keep the curl and volume."

Following the conclusion of Love On Tour, the singer sent shock waves through his fandom in November 2023 when he debuted a buzz cut at a U2 concert in Las Vegas. Not only did Stylers get their first look at Harry's shaved head, but also his rumored new girlfriend, actress Taylor Russell.

REAL ESTATE PORTFOLIO

At the age of eighteen, Harry went from his mother's modest home in Holmes Chapel to a four-bedroom mansion in North London when he signed a multimillion-dollar deal with One Direction—and has been moving on up ever since. He actually still owns his first piece of real estate, Erskine House, which he purchased in 2012 for £3.2 million ($4.5 million). The four-bedroom residence offers plenty of privacy, sitting behind a high wall and gates, as well as close proximity to a local attraction: The Spaniards Inn, a historic pub where Harry's been spotted on several occasions. In 2019, he snapped up a $10.9-million Georgian-style home with five bedrooms across the street. The following year, he expanded his portfolio with the residence next door, a $5.5-million eighteenth-century villa originally part of the same property—which suggested future plans for a mega "Harry's House."

Across the pond, the Brit first put down roots in Beverly Hills, with a 1960s Zen treehouse-style estate he purchased for $4 million in 2014. The three thousand-square-foot (279 m²) main house was a California dream: nestled in a lush landscape, with floor-to-ceiling picture windows for ultimate views of the surrounding canyons, bridged walkways, sunken courtyard, infinity saltwater pool, and guest bungalow. Two years later, Harry sold the property—which was sadly demolished for a new, modern home—and headed to the Hollywood Hills. Perched above the famed Sunset Strip, the $6.9-million remodeled 1947 three-story property features disappearing glass walls that open onto terraces for outdoor dining and sweeping panoramic views of the Pacific Ocean and downtown Los Angeles skyline. Harry also added his personal upgrade: a high-end audio system. Only a year later did he put the mansion on the market, yet he didn't sell it until 2019, and at a loss of $900,000, no less.

By that time, Harry had fallen out of love with the West Coast. "I feel like my relationship with LA has changed a lot," he told *Variety* in 2020. "I've kind of accepted that I don't have to live here anymore; for a while, I felt like I was supposed to. Like, it meant things were going well. This happened, and then you move to LA! But I don't really want to."

On the East Coast, he found the complete opposite: a nineteenth-century brick factory converted into luxury living in New York's Tribeca neighborhood. In 2017, Harry purchased the penthouse for $8.7 million—worth every penny for the priceless amenities like an indoor pool, Turkish baths, twenty-four-hour doorman, and concierge. For Harry and his famous neighbors, Justin Timberlake and Jennifer Lawrence, the building is practically paparazzi-proof: an underground garage ushers tenants to a private elevator that opens into their own home. Upstairs on

the seventh floor, Harry's three thousand-square-foot (279 m²) space has an industrial feel with an open-floor plan, flooded with natural light from the western-facing arched windows and stainless-steel kitchen.

STAR OF THE SCREEN

Just as Harry was launching his solo career, he also tapped into another talent: acting. In 2016, the singer was cast in Christopher Nolan's *Dunkirk*, a World War II epic about British soldiers awaiting rescue in Nazi-occupied France. Harry sought out the project, submitting an audition video that convinced the director that he was right for the part of Alex, the sole survivor of a German ambush. "He has an old-fashioned face," Nolan told the *Daily Mail*, "the kind of face that makes you believe he could have been alive in that period. Harry's character is very unglamorous. It's not a showboating role."

Harry agreed that playing Alex was "physically very tough" as it called for long hours submerged in freezing cold seawater. He gave a genuine performance, he confessed, because as an inexperienced actor, he could relate to the young soldiers who were trapped on Dunkirk's beach in 1940. "I think always being a little bit nervous when I was filming helped me," he told *The Sun*. "Any tension I felt personally helped the character." Critics hailed Harry's debut, with the Associated Press predicting the pop star "might just have another viable career option."

It would be a few more years before his next role—which was kept a secret from the public until the film's world premiere. In fact, it wasn't until the end of the 2021 Marvel superhero flick, *Eternals*, that his character, Eros, popped up in a mid-credits scene, shocking moviegoers who immediately spread the news on social media. Introduced as "the mighty Starfox," Eros is the half-brother of supervillain Thanos, responsible for killing half of the Marvel Cinematic Universe with a snap of his fingers in 2018's *Avengers: Infinity War*. In the comics, Eros and Thanos represent Desire and Death, with Harry's character able to stimulate the pleasure centers of people's brains, arousing them to the point of sedation. *Eternals* director, Chloé Zhao, "a giant Harry Styles fan," became obsessed with casting him, revealed Marvel executive Nate Moore on the *Crew Call* podcast. The famous singer's cameo was no stunt, however—Harry signed a deal to play Eros in five films. "There are more stories to be told with that character. He's fascinating," said Moore. "Having met Harry Styles, he is as charming as you think you want him to be. And I think there's no limit to how popular that character's gonna be once we get to bring him back."

In September 2022, he had two movies in theaters at the same time: *Don't Worry Darling* and *My Policeman*. The first, a psychological thriller, stars Harry and Florence Pugh as a married couple living in an idyllic mid-century desert community—although things are not what they seem. *Don't Worry Darling*, directed by Harry's then-girlfriend Olivia Wilde, opened to a mostly female audience, likely due to the singer's influence.

My Policeman, also set in the 1950s, showed much more of Harry's range as an actor, playing a closeted law enforcement officer in a small English town. Although reviews were mixed, critics saw his potential. As the *San Francisco Chronicle* put it: "After two films as a leading man, it's clear that Styles is more than a handsome face."

"After two films as a leading man, it's clear that Styles is more than a handsome face."

TRANSCENDENTAL MEDITATION

Harry balances out his hectic schedule with a relaxation technique that's also the go-to for Oprah Winfrey, Jennifer Aniston, Paul McCartney, Hugh Jackman, and Katy Perry. Twice a day, he sits in a quiet room and practices Transcendental Meditation (TM), which "allows the active thinking mind to settle inward to experience a naturally calm, peaceful level of awareness," according to the Center for Resilience of the David Lynch Foundation,

"That moment where you really let yourself be in that zone of being vulnerable, you reach this feeling of openness."

where Harry learned TM. During each twenty-minute session, "the body enjoys a profoundly rejuvenating rest, while the brain functions with significantly greater coherence."

Harry was introduced to TM by one of his best friends, music producer Tom Hull (aka Kid Harpoon), whom the singer calls "my emotional rock." Admittedly, he was a skeptic going into it, but became a believer once he noticed the benefits to his mental health. "I think meditation has helped with worrying about the future less, and the past less," he explained to *Rolling Stone*. "I feel like I take a lot more in—things that used to pass by me because I was always rushing around. It's part of being more open and talking with friends . . . But that moment where you really let yourself be in that zone of being vulnerable, you reach this feeling of openness."

Harry's such a believer in the benefits of meditation that he partnered with the Calm app to help fans find their inner peace. In 2020, the singer narrated "Dream With Me," a thirty-minute bedtime story intended to lull listeners to sleep with the dulcet tones of his voice, "the perfect tonic to calm a racing mind," noted Calm cofounder, Michael Acton Smith. Stylers were so eager to hear what Harry had to say that they crashed the app on the first day. As soft piano music played, he gently described a picturesque landscape as if he and the listener were enjoying the scene together. In one vignette, he narrated: "We find ourselves upon the shoreline, lounging by a lake. All crickets chirp in nearby reeds. It's hard to stay awake. The scene feels like a watercolor, soft diluted tones, as looking down we see each other laughing, skimming stones."

UNRELEASED MUSIC

Between 1D and his solo career, Harry has recorded well over a hundred songs—but there are dozens more which he's yet to officially release. Back in 2015, it was reported he had registered eight songs with ASCAP, yet not one of them appeared on his debut album, *Harry Styles*. Over the years since, outtakes from all three albums have made their way to social media. In 2023, a treasure trove leaked onto TikTok and Discord (and eventually ended up on YouTube and Soundcloud), with titles such as "High Tide," "Jesus Christ Happy New Year," "Make My Day," and "Try Honey."

Some of the unreleased songs have even made their way to Harry's set list, like fan-favorite "Medicine," which he recorded for 2017's *Harry Styles* and performed live several times, including at Coachella. Considered to be a rock 'n' roll LGBTQ+ anthem, many were disappointed when the banger didn't end up on *Fine Line* or *Harry's House*. "I think sonically it's just not really where I'm at anymore," Harry explained to Howard Stern in 2022. "I don't know that I'd go backward in that way by including a much older song. Maybe it'll make it on an album someday."

One of the most recent leaks in January 2024 circulated "Too Much Sauce," which became a hot topic as fans argued whether it was an outtake from *Harry's House* or actually meant for his upcoming fourth album.

VOMIT SHRINE

On October 12, 2014, Harry did something so relatable that a niche group of fans don't want to soon forget—he threw up on the side of the road. Paparazzi in Los Angeles captured the twenty-year-old exiting a chauffeured vehicle along the 101 Freeway and vomiting behind a guardrail. Within hours, a local Directioner named Gabrielle Kopera found the exact spot and taped up a poster that announced to passing motorists: "Harry Styles threw up here 10-12-14."

Initial reports claimed Harry had been partying the night before with British singer Lily Allen and was likely hungover. But he clarified on BBC Radio 1, "I'd been on a hike. I'd been on a very long hike"—which makes sense as he was wearing workout clothes in the photos. What did he think about the vomit shrine? "It's interesting for sure," Harry said with a shrug on *The Graham Norton Show* in 2017.

He was more concerned, however, that another fan went to the shrine to collect the infamous vomit—and tried to sell it on eBay. "It's worrying this is the world we live in," he told BBC Radio 1 at the time. But looking back three years later, he took the fan quirk in stride. "My mom actually sent me, like, an eBay link to my own puke, which was very interesting to receive on a Tuesday morning," Harry joked to NPR.

WALKING TOUR OF HOLMES CHAPEL

Those who want to retrace Harry's path to stardom can explore the hometown where it all began: Holmes Chapel in Cheshire, England. After years of superfans descending on the quaint village, in 2023, the Holmes Chapel Partnership (HCP) issued a map with "safe walking routes" to several local landmarks following footpaths, country lanes, and pedestrian bridges. The most popular point of interest is Twemlow Viaduct, known to Stylers as "Harry's Wall," the site of his first kiss. In the 1D documentary, *This Is Us*, he visited the spot and wrote his name on its brick facade—which has encouraged fans to do the same, despite HCP's warning that "to deface it with graffiti is a criminal offense."

From there, it's a twenty-minute walk to Picton Square for a sweet treat at W. Mandeville Bakery, where he worked for two years before becoming an overnight sensation with One Direction. Fans can even pose next to a life-size image of teenage Harry, clad in a maroon apron and holding up a loaf of bread. Other Harry hotspots include his favorite Chinese restaurant, Fortune City, and Hermitage Primary School.

HCP suggests that fans who visit Harry's hometown take the train from Manchester City Centre, south of Holmes Chapel station, approximately a forty-minute trip.

"I got such a thrill when
I was in front of people singing.
It made me want to do it
more and more."

X FACTOR AUDITION

Harry's big break was captured by *The X Factor* cameras, beginning with the very moment the sixteen-year-old arrived to audition for the reality TV competition in 2010. Waiting around outside the venue, he was approached by host Dermot O'Leary, who asked, "What sort of experience have you got music-wise?" Harry bragged about his then-band, White Eskimo, and said that performing for their small fanbase back in Holmes Chapel "really showed me that's what I wanted to do. I got such a thrill when I was in front of people singing. It made me want to do it more and more." If *X Factor* judges didn't think he had the necessary talent to compete on the show, Harry admitted it would be "a major setback in my plans."

Cameras then followed him backstage as he prepared to go before Simon Cowell, Nicole Scherzinger, and Louis Walsh. His family and friends—all decked out in shirts that say "We Think Harry Has the X Factor"—gave him good-luck kisses as he headed off for the audition that would change his life.

After the episode aired in September 2010, a clip of Harry's audition was uploaded to YouTube, where it amassed over twenty-six million views. In 2022, *The X Factor* added an extended version with never-before-seen footage of the future superstar bantering with the judges and singing Train's "Hey Soul Sister."

YOUTH SPELL

Becoming a global heartthrob at the tender age of sixteen changed the way Harry looked at a lot of things, especially since he's gotten older. He admitted he "had a moment" when seventeen-year-old Billie Eilish first blew up with "Bad Guy" in 2019—he not only reflected on who he had been with One Direction, but more so who he wanted to become as an adult artist. Without youth, "how do you play that game of remaining exciting," Harry, twenty-eight, mused to Zane Lowe in 2022. Ultimately, he made peace with the past by envisioning "who I would like to be as a musician . . . She totally broke the [youth] spell for me in a way that I'm very grateful for."

Harry and Billie have crossed paths many times over the years, most memorably at the 2021 *Grammys* as the two cheered on each other's wins—even when "Watermelon Sugar" beat her "Everything I Wanted" for Best Pop Solo Performance. Yet he had never confessed to Billie how her influence liberated his artistry. "I just want to make good music," Harry explained to Lowe. "That's it. That's what I want to do. And everything else is what it will be. And that's kind of it."

Interestingly, Harry has had the same effect on Billie. She was one of the estimated one hundred thousand in the crowd for his 2022 Coachella performance and was inspired by his bravery to debut several tracks from *Harry's House*.

Two months later, during a concert in Manchester, she performed "TV," a song she had just written with her brother, Finneas, about women losing constitutional rights in the US. "I was thinking, 'Wow, that's so cool.' He's such a big deal, and playing an unreleased song really opens the floodgates of all these questions: Will people shit on it? Will they hate it? Will they love it? Will it be a thing? Will they get bored of it? Will somebody steal it?" Billie mused to Lowe in her own Apple Music 1 interview. "It's really vulnerable to play a song that is not out that is that vulnerable to you, and that's what I wanted to do."

ZIGGY STARDUST

One of Harry's greatest musical influences is David Bowie, specifically the British icon's early 1970s alter ego, Ziggy Stardust, an androgynous alien rock star who personified glam rock with a flaming red-orange mullet and flamboyant stage costumes. Bowie introduced the fictional character on his fifth album, *The Rise and Fall of Ziggy Stardust and the Spiders from Mars*, which was released in 1972. Its lead single, "Starman," prophesied the second coming of a mysterious extraterrestrial who will offer salvation to young earthlings.

"Now I'll put on something that feels really flamboyant, and I don't feel crazy wearing it."

Ziggy came to life on Bowie's subsequent world tour, and by the time he returned to England for the final leg in June 1973, Ziggymania had invaded the planet: Album and concert ticket sales solidified him as the biggest English rock star since the Beatles a decade earlier. "Everybody started to treat me as they treated Ziggy: as though I were the Next Big Thing, as though I moved masses of people," Bowie recalled to *Rolling Stone* in 1974. "I became convinced I was a messiah. Very scary. I woke up fairly quickly." He retired the character on the last night of the Ziggy Stardust Tour.

Just as Harry is Gucci's fashion muse, Ziggy Stardust was exclusively dressed in custom stage costumes by Kansai Yamamoto, the first Japanese designer to show in London. Among the most memorable outfits was "Tokyo Pop," a vinyl jumpsuit with exaggerated bell legs, and the "Woodland Creatures" shorts romper adorned with rabbits that "live on the moon," according to Japanese mythology. Five decades later, Harry's Love On Tour look mimicked Ziggy's iconic style, with feather boas, bell-bottoms, bright reds and oranges, and lots of sequins. Looking up to a "showman" like Bowie emboldened Harry's fashion choices, he told *Vogue*. "Now I'll put on something that feels really flamboyant, and I don't feel crazy wearing it."

Musically, Bowie's alter ego impacted Harry on *Fine Line* as he let go of the fears that held him back creatively on his debut album—and felt emboldened to just be himself. "It was really joyous and really free," Harry told *Vogue*. "I think with music it's so important to evolve—and that extends to clothes and videos and all that stuff. That's why you look back at David Bowie with Ziggy Stardust or the Beatles and their different eras—that fearlessness is super inspiring."

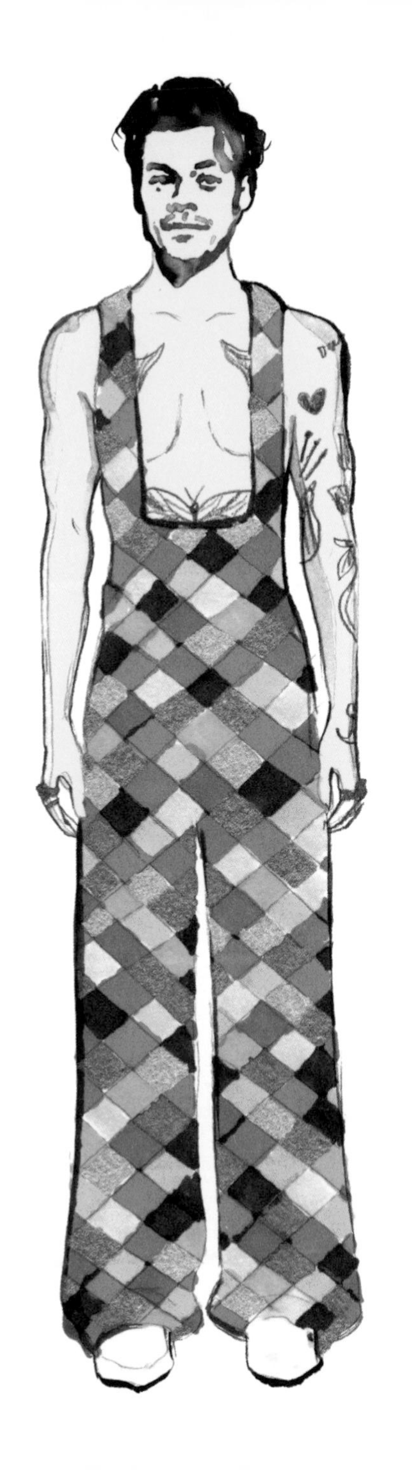

PART FOUR

Pop Culture Shift

INCLUSIVE KING

Of all of Harry's endless accolades, what he's most proud of is bringing people together—people from all walks of life—at his sold-out shows around the world. For ninety minutes each night, someone can be their authentic selves, free of judgment and full of acceptance, in an emotionally generous atmosphere. A Harry Styles concert is a safe place for anyone who might feel uncomfortable in society because of what they look like, how they dress, who they love, or the color of their skin. All they have to do is look up and see a rainbow Pride flag draped over Harry's mic stand or a Black Lives Matter sticker on his guitar.

"I get kind of a front-row seat to see a bunch of people getting in a room together and just being themselves," Harry explained to *Dazed* in 2021. "Dancing like nobody's watching. Having the most basic version of a good time. Humans interacting and accepting each other. A room full of people just loving each other is so powerful."

As far back as 2014, Harry's been an ally of the LGBTQ+ community—which has raised questions about his own sexuality. Asked in an interview what One Direction looks for in a girlfriend, Liam Payne joked "female." "Not that important," Harry confessed with a shrug. Earlier that year, at a 1D concert in St. Louis, Missouri, he wore Michael Sam's football jersey in support of the NFL's first openly gay player.

Later, during his solo world tours, many LGBTQ+ fans felt emboldened to come out to their families with Harry's help. One of the first times was in 2018 when a young woman named Grace held up a sign telling the singer she had traveled 2,846 miles (4,580 km) to attend his San Jose, California, concert. On the back, she added, "I'm gonna come out to my parents because of you!!!" When he learned Grace's mother was back in the hotel room, he instructed the entire arena to shout "Tina, she's gay!" loud enough for her to hear. After the show, Grace showed her mother a video of the moment. Not only was Tina "overjoyed," tweeted Grace, "she wants to thank Harry for helping me come out."

In 2018, Harry coined a slogan that has become the mantra of his fandom: "Treat people with kindness." During Live On Tour, those four words adorned a pin on his guitar strap, grabbing the attention of Stylers who gravitated to its universal message and adopted it as their own. That inspired Harry to put out a limited-edition line of TPWK merchandise in 2018, with proceeds going to the Gay, Lesbian & Straight Education

But Harry admits, like many of his fans, he's still figuring it out himself.

Network, an organization that raises awareness about protecting LGBTQ+ youth in schools.

As TPWK spread love across the world, Harry immortalized the motto with a tribute song, "Treat People with Kindness," a gospel-rock track off his 2019 album, *Fine Line*. "A big part of the freedom that I felt making this record came from touring last time and the interaction with the fans . . . [they] want me to make the music that I want to make and play the show that I'd like to play," he explained to *Music Week*. "People just want me to be myself and be authentic with them." And he encouraged them to feel the same.

After breaking barriers with his gender-fluid fashion, in 2021 Harry launched Pleasing, a gender-neutral beauty line of nail polishes and serums that celebrates "the multitude of unique identities in our community." Over the years, it has evolved into cosmetics, fragrances, apparel, and accessories. "I also think that what this can become is so much more than just products you can buy," Harry predicted to *Dazed*. "I think it's about giving and giving back. I am blessed to have fans who are so supportive of me, who believe in freedom, and who have created this safe space for each other. Pleasing is really for them. That feeling of community is kind of what we would like Pleasing to reflect."

While the media has tried in vain to put a label on Harry, he has held firm to ambiguity. However, his refusal to confirm his own sexuality has drawn accusations of queerbaiting LGBQT+ audiences. But Harry admits, like many of his fans, he's still figuring it out himself. "I've been really open with it with my friends, but that's my personal experience; it's mine," he confessed to *Better Homes & Gardens*. "The whole point of where we should be heading, which is toward accepting everybody and being more open, is that it doesn't matter, and it's about not having to label everything, not having to clarify what boxes you're checking."

MALE FEMINIST

The demographic of Harry's fan base skews female and young—and the girl power has been his driving force. Even as a teenager in his One Direction days, when the boy band was asked about hooking up with fans, the singer would call out the unfair objectification. In 2017, while promoting his debut solo album, he proudly donned a shirt proclaiming, "Women are smarter." He doubled down in interviews, explaining why young females, especially, are a barometer for good music. "They're the most honest . . . They have that bullshit detector," Harry told *Rolling Stone*. "We're so past that dumb outdated narrative of 'Oh, these people are girls, so they don't know what they're talking about.' They're the ones who *know* what they're talking about." Respecting women comes naturally to Harry because he was raised by a single mother with an older sister, so he doesn't get why the concept is hard for some to grasp. "People think that if you say, 'I'm a feminist,' it means you think men should burn in hell and women should trample on their necks. No, you think women should be equal. That doesn't feel like a crazy thing to me."

FASHION REVOLUTION

As one of five talents in One Direction, Harry had to find creative ways to stand out among the group. Early on, he revealed flashes of his bold sense of style: floral prints and blouses with skinny jeans and ankle boots. His risk-taking earned Harry the distinction of being 2013's most stylish at the British Fashion Awards, beating out veterans Kate Middleton, Kate Moss, and David Beckham. Once the singer joined forces with stylist Harry Lambert, he entered his "Jagger period," rocking flashier suits and silk scarves à la the Rolling Stones frontman.

"I think what's exciting about right now is you can wear what you like. It doesn't have to be X or Y. Those lines are becoming more and more blurred."

As a solo artist, Harry's flamboyant fashion became an extension of his creativity. The week his debut album dropped, he stepped out to promote it in a parade of high-fashion suits: bespoke candy pink, red-and-white plaid, brown mohair with embroidered dragons. For his first solo tour, in the fall of 2017, Harry hit the road in one-of-a-kind Gucci pieces designed by creative director Alessandro Michele: a harlequin suit with a sheer bow blouse in Las Vegas; floral-printed velvet in San Francisco; metallic silk jacquard for New York's Radio City Music Hall. By creating an audiovisual experience for fans, he was also making a fashion statement—he's nothing like his male pop-star contemporaries.

For his second album, 2019's *Fine Line*, Harry took a literal interpretation with his style. He pushed the boundaries even further, particularly with gender-fluid accessories, such as a pearl necklace, clutch purse, crochet driving gloves, and faux-fur boas in an array of colors. Pairing the masculine with the feminine, Harry embodied rock-star chic, even if his fashion choices were sometimes controversial. In December 2020, he made history as the first man to grace the cover of American *Vogue* solo—in a dress, no less. "When you take away 'There's clothes for men and there's clothes for women,' once you remove any barriers, obviously you open up the arena in which you can play," he explained in the magazine. "I'll go in shops sometimes, and I just find myself looking at the women's clothes thinking they're amazing. It's like anything—anytime you're putting barriers up in your own life, you're just limiting yourself."

Some critics seemed perfectly happy to live in their tiny bubble. Conservative commentator Candace Owens unleashed on social media, bemoaning the "steady feminization of our men . . . Bring back manly men." As his fans went after Owens in the comments, Harry silenced her by reclaiming her intended insult. "Bring back manly men," the singer captioned a photo of himself in a powder blue suit with pleated flared sleeves, from his *Variety* Hitmaker of the Year shoot. In the accompanying cover story, he expressed no regrets for dressing as he pleased. "I think what's exciting about right now is you can wear what you like. It doesn't have to be X or Y. Those lines are becoming more and more blurred."

By 2022's *Harry's House*, he was loud and proud: The year's fashion was defined by lots of pink, sequins, neon, bell sleeves, and pinstripes. Harry also went from muse to designer, with his own 1970s-inspired Gucci line with Alessandro, HA HA HA (their first initials), a whimsical collection of clothing and accessories adorned with cherries, hearts, squirrels, and teddy bears. "Harry has an incredible sense of fashion," praised his good friend and Gucci's creative director. "I proposed creating a 'dream wardrobe' with him, starting from those small oddities that come together in childlike visions. We ended up with a mix of aesthetics from 1970s pop and bohemian to the revision of the image of the gentleman in an overturned memory of men's tailoring."

HA HA HA was no joke. Most of the twenty-five items, which ranged in price from $235 to $4,200, sold out. That was music to the ears of Gucci executives who announced plans to boost the company's 2023 annual sales by "introducing young millennials and Gen Z to the luxury sector."

With or without fancy clothes, Harry has empowered his millions of fans to be their most authentic selves in whatever makes them comfortable—by paving the way with his own individuality. "It's the vibe shift," his stylist, Harry Lambert, told *The Guardian*. "When I'm gone, I just hope it's silly things such as putting Harry in pearls and that men can wear necklaces and it not be a thing . . . It means that we've done something that has had a cultural impact. It means we've got through."

PROFILES OF STYLES

Harry's most iconic looks have been immortalized in wax at Madame Tussauds museums around the world—with seven unveiled on the same day in 2023. New York and Berlin celebrate the singer's Coachella costumes, rainbow-sequined jumpsuit and faux-fur coat over metallic leather pants, respectively. Harry's Love On Tour was just as memorable for its fashion and some of his greatest hits are on replay at museum locations: In Amsterdam, it's the pink, double-breasted suit with floral embroidery from his Dallas, Texas, concert; Sydney salutes the pink satin shirt, burgundy trousers, and boa Harry rocked in San Jose, California; in Singapore, the sweet strawberry-adorned two-piece from the Glasgow show is exhibited. Harry's tattoos take center stage in Hollywood, where his wax figure is draped in the gold sequin fringed vest from his historic fifteen-night run at Madison Square Garden. In London—where the One Direction heartthrob's first wax figure debuted in 2013 with Liam, Louis, Niall, and Zayn—his solo statue commemorates his film career, with the green Gucci suit and matching purse from the premiere for *My Policeman*.

DRESSED TO THRILL

With the last name Styles, Harry was born to be a fashion icon. "As a kid, I definitely liked fancy dress," he revealed to *Vogue*. And as one of the biggest pop stars on the planet, that authentic flamboyance has challenged society's views on masculinity. "There's so much joy to be had in playing with clothes. I've never really thought too much about what it means—it just becomes this extended part of creating something." Here are some of Harry's most memorable works of wearable art.

SHEAR GENIUS

As cochair of the 2019 *Met Gala*, Harry took the night's theme quite seriously. To him, Camp: Notes on Fashion meant wearing something that elicits "enjoyment and fun, no judgment." And that's just what he achieved in an all-black Gucci sheer pussy-bow blouse, high-waisted trousers, and patent-leather heels—with a nontraditional accessory: a single pearl earring. Most surprisingly, Harry did not have pierced ears at the time, so he did it himself with a needle days before the main event, when his stylist, Harry Lambert, spotted the bauble, a bee with crystal wings and oblong pearl drop, on Gucci's site and knew "it was the perfect final touch for the outfit."

TECHNICOLOR DREAM

The *Harry's House* era established him as "King of the Jumpsuits," with variations characterized by sequins, stripes, fringe, polka dots, and hearts. For his big night at the 2023 *Grammys*—where the singer was up for six awards—Harry elevated the trend with a harlequin-patterned rainbow one-piece adorned with 250,000 Swarovski crystals in nine different colors for a glittery effect. The unique custom piece is "a visual metaphor for his personality, his commitment to self-expression, and total acceptance," described French fashion brand EgonLab. "It is like a window to another world, a world of pure magic and wonder."

DISCO KING

For his first time performing at Coachella in 2022, Harry dazzled onstage—literally. Gucci created a multicolored mirror-detailed look that essentially turned the singer into a human disco ball for an electric set

The ***Harry's House*** *era established him as "King of the Jumpsuits."*

that included the debut of several new tracks off *Harry's House*. Ever the trendsetter, Harry's snazzy two-piece (which seamlessly blended together to appear like a one-piece) sparked an e-commerce demand for "rainbow sequin jumpsuits" that leaped 3,233 percent, according to UK fast-fashion retailer Pretty Little Thing. On TikTok, #HarryStylesOutfit went viral with 18.4 million views.

BRIGHT AND EARLY

Decked out in head-to-toe fluorescent stripes, Harry woke up America in style for an early morning concert on the *Today* show in 2022. The 1970s-inspired JW Anderson jumpsuit with bell sleeves and flared legs lit up social media, dividing fans on what the bold pattern reminded them of—a candy cane or black swallowtail caterpillar. But most could agree he was a ray of sunshine on the gray, drizzly morning. "It's early, so I wanted to be comfortable," explained Harry. "And I thought I could soak up some of the rain with this."

GENERATIONAL GAP

Harry's musical heroes had their heyday long before he was born. But good songwriting is timeless, and baby boomers like Fleetwood Mac, the Beatles, the Rolling Stones, David Bowie, and Queen have shaped every aspect of the millennial's artistry, from his songwriting and showmanship to fashion—and in return, he's introduced younger generations to the musical pioneers who paved his way.

STEVIE NICKS

Like Harry, the Fleetwood Mac singer took a major risk when she left the group to go solo in 1981 with *Bella Donna*, which spawned several hits including "Edge of Seventeen." The two first connected in 2015 when the One Direction singer surprised Nicks backstage at London's O2 Arena with a cake for her sixty-seventh birthday.

Describing Harry as "very old school, but modern," she praised his decision to make a rock 'n' roll album. "He could have made a pop record and that would have been the easy way for him," she told *Rolling Stone*. "But I guess he decided he wanted to be born in 1948, too—he made a record that was more like 1975." And when he finished his second album, *Fine Line*, Nicks was one of the first to hear it. The seventy-year-old showed up with a group of girlfriends and stayed until after 3 a.m. Harry recalled the early-morning hang with the "little witches coven" to Howard Stern: "I'm like, 'I'm kinda tired' and they're right in their prime. They're really like, 'Oh, this is like daytime for us.'"

Over the years, Harry and Nicks have shared many unforgettable moments onstage. In 2017, she joined her "little muse" at the Troubadour on the Sunset Strip in Los Angeles for renditions of Fleetwood Mac's "Landslide" and Nick's "Leather and Lace." The following year, Harry teamed up with a reunited Fleetwood Mac for a performance of the 1977 classic "The Chain."

When Nicks was inducted into the Rock & Roll Hall of Fame in 2019, Harry honored his "magical gypsy godmother" by detailing her influence: "I hope she knows what she means to us, what she means to yet another generation of artists who look to her for inspiration and trailblazing courage."

PAUL MCCARTNEY

One of Harry's most significant musical heroes, the Beatles singer-turned-solo-artist has been a sounding board for the millennial superstar. In 2017, he got the opportunity to interview McCartney for *Another Man* magazine and picked his brain about transitioning from a group.

When the Beatles broke up in 1970, McCartney had wondered if he should make similar-sounding music or go in a totally different direction. Ultimately, he chose the second option and started a new band, Wings, with his wife Linda and former Moody Blues guitarist, Denny Laine. McCartney explained to Harry that he made it a point to write music the Beatles never would have done. It wasn't until Wings' third album, *Band on the Run*, that "I thought it was okay to do Beatles stuff again because I'd proved my point to myself. These days I do lots of Beatles things, it doesn't matter anymore, I'm happy to do anything. But at first, it was a little bit difficult, I must admit."

Speaking from his own experience, Harry explained to McCartney that he didn't come out of One Direction "feeling like I wasn't able to do what I wanted to do. I loved it." Unlike the Beatles legend, Harry added several 1D songs to the setlist for his first solo tour, including their first hit "What Makes You Beautiful" and deep cut "Stockholm Syndrome"—both of which he reprised for Love On Tour.

MICK JAGGER

Five decades before Harry bent gender norms, the Rolling Stones frontman put androgynous fashion on the map. In 2016, comparisons between the two hit a fevered pitch when Harry was reportedly in talks to portray Jagger in a biopic based on the making of their album *Exile on Main Street*. He even gave a preview of his impersonation of the rock star in a 2017 *Saturday Night Live* skit.

"I like Harry, we have an easy relationship."

But after several years of delays, the film was ultimately stalled. That might have come as a relief to Jagger, who disagreed with the Harry comparison in a 2022 interview with the *Times*. "I like Harry, we have an easy relationship," he said. "[But] I mean, I used to wear a lot more eye makeup than him. Come on, I was much more androgynous. And he doesn't have a voice like mine or move on stage like me; he just has a superficial resemblance to my younger self, which is fine—he can't help that."

FREDDIE MERCURY

Harry has drawn comparisons to the electric Queen frontman since his solo debut, "Sign of the Times," and it came full circle when he had his own "Freddie Mercury moment" during a 2022 concert at London's Wembley Stadium. Thirty-seven years after the rock band played the Live Aid charity concert—hailed as the greatest live performance of all time—Harry paid tribute to Mercury's iconic vocal volley with the audience.

Back in 1985, following "Radio Ga Ga," Mercury had led the seventy-two thousand in attendance in a sing-along of "ay-ohhh" runs, immortalized in the final sequence of the 2018 blockbuster *Bohemian Rhapsody*, starring Rami Malek. When Harry's Love On Tour came to Wembley in 2022, the enigmatic singer pumped up the crowd à la Mercury with a similar vocal exercise.

JONI MITCHELL

While making *Fine Line*, "I was in a big Joni hole," admitted Harry. In particular, he was obsessed with the folk singer's *Blue*, widely considered one of the greatest albums of all time. To Harry, the 1971 masterpiece exploring Michell's relationships with Graham Nash and James Taylor is "just the ultimate in terms of songwriting." Musically, what jumped out at him was its use of the dulcimer, a fretted string instrument, typically with three or four strings. Eager to capture the same sound on *Fine Line*, he tracked down the woman who built Mitchell's in the 1960s. She invited the young singer into her Los Angeles home—and even taught him how to play the eighteenth-century instrument. "Then she got a bongo and we were all jamming with these big Cheshire Cat grins," recalled Harry's songwriting partner, Tom Hull (aka Kid Harpoon).

His next album, *Harry's House*, also hints at Mitchell's influence—she has a song of the same name, off 1975's *The Hissing of Summer Lawns*. Mitchell was flattered: "love the title," she tweeted to Harry in March 2022. As it turned out, he had been to Joni's house for a star-studded Christmas sing-along he described as "one of the more nerve-racking moments in my life." Brandi Carlile, a ten-time Grammy winner, volunteered Harry to sing Mitchell's "River" in front of the legend, no less. Stage fright aside, Harry admitted "it was pretty special."

In February 2024, just days after the octogenarian made history at her first-ever performance at the *Grammy Awards*, Mitchell celebrated the four-year anniversary of Harry's "sensational cover" of her 1970 classic "Big Yellow Taxi" by posting the video on social media with the caption "Love was in the air."

CAROLE KING

When Harry played back *Fine Line* for the first time ever, he did so in a sacred place: The same room where Carole King had recorded her own second album, 1971's *Tapestry*, which produced the classics "It's Too Late" and "I Feel the Earth Move." Four decades later, he stood in Studio B at the former A&M Studios (now Henson Recording Studios) in Hollywood hosting an exclusive group who would hear his completed sophomore album from start to finish. When King read the revelation in *Rolling Stone*, she reposted the article on social media for her fans to read with a special note: "Thanks, Harry Styles. I love that we have Studio B in common."

HARRY NILSSON

Considering how much Harry loves the Beatles, it's no surprise he gravitates to one of the Fab Four's favorite artists. Harry Nilsson, sometimes referred to as "The American Beatle," befriended the band and even collaborated with John Lennon, whose 1980 murder made him step away from music to campaign for gun control.

Nilsson died two weeks before Harry was born, yet his legacy lives on: While the former One Direction singer was working on his solo debut, "I listened to a lot of Harry Nilsson," he told *Rolling Stone*. "His lyrics are honest and so good, and I think it's because he's never trying to sound clever."

That was exactly what Harry was going for on his second album, and he leaned into his appreciation of Nilsson. Citing Nilsson's 1971 novelty song, "Coconut," Harry felt "so much less afraid to write fun pop songs" on *Fine Line*.

"For the memories you gave me with my mother, I will be forever grateful."

SHANIA TWAIN

While Harry's father introduced him to classic rock, his mother shared her favorite contemporary music during his childhood—and on regular rotation was Twain's 1997 country-pop *Come on Over*, the biggest-selling studio album of all time by a solo female artist.

Decades later, she met "sweet" Harry backstage at one of his concerts and he gushed about how much he loved his mother Anne for making him a fan. He had just one request: Could she call Anne on her upcoming birthday? Twain happily obliged, and thus began a beautiful friendship that led to her joining Harry onstage at Coachella in 2022 for a surprise duet of her chart-toppers "Man! I Feel Like a Woman!" and "You're Still the One." It was a full-circle moment for Harry. "In the car with my mother as a child, this lady taught me to sing," he told the audience. "For the memories you gave me with my mother, I will be forever grateful." The revitalized interest in her music inspired Twain to record *Queen of Me* in 2023 and opened the door for a future collaboration with her most famous fan. It's been discussed, she revealed to *Extra*, and "I'm going to hold Harry to that."

AMERICAN IDOL

Harry may be British, but he's concerned with global matters. In the United States specifically, where he has millions of fans, the singer has taken a vested interest in current events and social policies. His concern began with the 2016 presidential election of Donald Trump, whose platform aimed to strip the rights of women and gay/transgender people—inspiring Harry to write "Sign of the Times." "That's me commenting on different things . . . just the state of the world at the moment," he told the *New York Times* in 2017. "It's very much me looking at that.

"I do things every day without fear,
because I am privileged,
and I am privileged every day
because I am white."

It's a time when it's very easy to feel incredibly sad about a lot of things. It's also nice sometimes to remember that while there's a lot of bad stuff, there's also a lot of amazing people doing amazing things in the world."

Harry put his money where his mouth was amid the 2020 Black Lives Matter movement protesting the death of George Floyd by white police officers in Minneapolis. The singer donated to a bail fund for arrested activists and encouraged his followers to also get involved in racial justice. "I do things every day without fear, because I am privileged, and I am privileged every day because I am white," Harry wrote on social media. "Being not racist is not enough, we must be anti-racist. Social change is enacted when a society mobilizes. I stand in solidarity with all those protesting . . . ENOUGH IS ENOUGH."

Three days later, he was spotted at a peaceful protest in Los Angeles, marching the streets for miles holding a sign that read "Black Lives Matter." In a photo posted by actor Al Shearer, Harry kneels on Hollywood's Sunset Boulevard with a fist raised. "Not even from this country, but puts his life on the line, his career on the line to back us up," Shearer captioned the powerful image.

That fall, President Trump went head-to-head against Democratic nominee Joe Biden in the 2020 election. A few years after Harry wrote "Sign of the Times," he had become much more demonstrative in calling for change. Instead of just singing about the issues, he rallied his thirty-five million followers on Twitter (now known as X): "If I could vote in America, I'd vote with kindness," he wrote alongside a campaign video of Biden. Voters seemingly heeded Harry's advice, with Millennials and Gen Zers turning out in record numbers. According to research conducted by Tufts University, 50 percent of young people (ages 18 to 29) voted in the 2020 election, with the majority supporting the victorious Biden.

Harry's Love On Tour brought goodwill to five continents, and in the US specifically, he promoted democracy and peace. The singer partnered with nonpartisan voter engagement organization HeadCount, encouraging fans to register to vote ahead of the 2022 midterm elections. The incentive was high: a chance to win travel and tickets to his annual Harryween concert in Los Angeles on Halloween Day. Within the first twenty-four hours, 28,760 fans registered to vote—a single-day record for HeadCount in its eighteen-year history. Over the following weeks, Harry pulled in 54,000 new voters, one-third of the organization's total registered voters in 2022. The fan who won the Harryween sweepstakes gushed to *People* magazine that she was "super proud to be a fan of someone like Harry who wants to make a change and encourage everyone to do better."

In Austin, Texas, Harry performed to a sold-out crowd of eighty-six thousand—and publicly endorsed Beto O'Rourke, the Democratic nominee for governor, with a "Beto for Texas" sticker adorning his guitar. "So many young people who weren't really plugged into this campaign—or really this race—or maybe didn't know there was an election taking place in Texas or the issues . . . they're taking notice," O'Rourke, who attended Harry's October 2 concert, told *Hysteria* podcast. "They're curious and they're coming out and they're getting registered to vote. So that was a huge boost, and I am so grateful to him."

SPREADING AWARENESS

The US leg of Love On Tour also put a spotlight on Everytown for Gun Safety, a nonprofit organization that advocates against gun violence. Days after a mass shooting at Robb Elementary School in Uvalde, Texas, killed nineteen children, an "absolutely devastated" Harry announced the partnership along with his pledge to donate $1 million to the Everytown for Gun Safety Support Fund. At forty-four concerts from Los Angeles to New York, volunteers from Students Demand Action spread awareness to fans—and the response was overwhelming. "People walking by were just so happy that we were there, happy that we were fighting for this cause, and really eager to sign up and learn more," Mia Tretta, an eighteen-year-old school shooting survivor, told *Teen Vogue*. Chloe Gayer, another volunteer, drove six hours to work at Harry's Chicago concert. She expressed appreciation to the British singer for "taking the time to stand with us. Even though it's a very controversial issue, he's using his platform to help save lives."

17BLACK
NY

TATTOO GUIDE

A firm believer in bodily autonomy and freedom of choice, it's no surprise Harry is covered in well over sixty tattoos. Each one holds sentimental value (for the most part), honoring his family, friends, exes, travels, personal experiences, and favorite things. With that many tattoos, naturally, there are a few he regrets, mostly those he allowed friends to put on his body—and one he even did himself! Some he has covered up, like "I can change," which he proved by camouflaging it with an anchor. This is the complete guide to Harry's tattoos, head to toe.

TORSO

There would be no Harry without his parents, Desmond Styles and Anne Twist, and he commemorates his father and mother with birth years, 1957 and 1967 respectively, tattooed on either side of his clavicle. Working outward to his shoulders, a cursive "A" near "1967" is also for Anne and mirrors a "G" on his right shoulder for his sister Gemma. Below the "A" on his chest reads "17 Black," the specific bet that made Harry lose a ton of money gambling while in Australia for One Direction's 2012 Up All Night Tour.

When Harry was eighteen, he made the bold decision to get inked with massive sparrows on each pectoral muscle, an area of the body particularly sensitive to a tattoo needle. "It hurt," he admitted to *Us Weekly* at the time. "I like that kind of style of tattoos, like the old sailor kind of tattoos. They symbolize traveling, and we travel a lot!" Soon after, he got an even bigger piece of permanent art, a massive black-and-white butterfly across his torso, his most iconic yet mysterious tattoo—some fans argue it's actually a moth. According to the artist Liam Sparks, Harry was inspired by the 1973 film *Papillon* (French for "butterfly"), which stars Steve McQueen as a safecracker with a similar tattoo on his chest.

Over his heart, fittingly there's half of a broken heart as well as two crosses with the letters "M" and "K," for his maternal grandmother, Mary, and paternal grandfather, Keith. On the opposite side of his chest, a lone identical cross bears a "B" for his paternal grandmother, Beryl.

Harry has not shied away from one of the most painful areas to get a tattoo: the bony ribcage. His largest is an empty birdcage, with the door closed. Next to it, he added a pair of theater masks—representing comedy and tragedy—which pairs well with the nearby acronym "SNCL"—"smile now, cry later."

"I like that kind of style of tattoos, like the old sailor kind of tattoos."

ARMS

The first tattoo Harry ever got was the outline of a star on his left bicep, which he later filled in with black ink. Nearby, there's a black heart, as well as an anatomical heart with gray shading to create dimension. Several of the pieces scattered on his left arm reflect a few of his favorite things: an acoustic guitar, the triangular prism from the cover of Pink Floyd's *Dark Side of the Moon* (One Direction's Zayn Malik and Louis Tomlinson have the same tattoo), a clothes hanger, and "Pingu" after the British animated series of the same name about a penguin. Harry also has abbreviations of the three cities where he has lived: New York, Los Angeles, and London. To remind the singer of his travels while on tour, he got an eighteenth-century warship in 2012 while accompanied by then-girlfriend Taylor Swift. Two years later, he added a similarly themed mermaid on his forearm.

Some tattoos seem random, like "Hi," "Silver Spoon," a handshake, a flying insect, a rose, a skeleton wearing a tuxedo, and "Late Late." The latter he got on the CBS' *The Late Late Show with James Corden* in 2015 after losing a game of Tattoo Roulette. Another one is the result of a bet he

Assuming the team would defeat their opponent, Harry just went ahead and got the ink, "and then they lost."

made on the Green Bay Packers, his favorite football team. If they won an upcoming game, "then I'll get a Packers tattoo," he promised a friend. Assuming the team would defeat their opponent, Harry just went ahead and got the ink, "and then they lost."

Several pay tribute to Harry's loved ones. He has a second, smaller "A" for his mother Anne in the crook of his left arm. Her late husband, Robin, is memorialized with an "R" on Harry's forearm, which he got a few months before he died from cancer in 2017. The singer illustrates his brotherly love for sister Gemma in two places on his left arm: an iced gem cookie (perhaps also a nod to his first job in a bakery) on the inside of his bicep and the Hebrew letters that spell her name on the outside. The siblings also have matching palm trees on their right triceps. Harry's late maternal grandmother is again honored with "Mary" on his right forearm. He even acknowledges his godsons, Jackson and Arlo, with their names written in script.

Around his wrist are several small tattoos: a three-leaf clover, a padlock, and a skeleton key (done by Ed Sheeran), an Aquarius symbol (his zodiac sign), and "99P" (99 pence). On top of his hand, between his thumb and index finger, is a tiny cross.

Although Harry considers himself "more spiritual than religious," he inked each of his forearms with a phrase from the Serenity Prayer: "God, grant me the serenity to accept the *things I cannot* change, the courage to change the *things I can*, and wisdom to know the difference." However, in 2015, he had a change of heart and covered up "Things I Cannot" with an eagle and "Things I Can" with a Bible.

LEGS

The least covered area of his body, his legs, the ink is all over the place, both literally and figuratively. On his left thigh is a giant tiger head and "Brasil!"—which he pulled down his pants to show fans onstage in Rio de Janeiro in 2015. On his right thigh is "Olivia," which fans first spotted in 2023, months after he broke up with Olivia Wilde. Above and below his kneecaps are the words "yes" and "no" written in French and Spanish.

FEET

As a reminder to stay grounded, Harry got a tiny "x" inked on his right ankle, along with One Direction members Zayn, Louis, and Liam (Niall remains tattoo-free). Another literal mark is "big" written on his left big toe, which he admitted is one of his "couple stupid ones." His right toe appears to be adorned with a crown. And where else would he put a tattoo about dancing? Harry's ankles read "Never Gonna" and "Dance Again" from the chorus of George Michael's 1984 ballad, "Careless Whisper."

ACKNOWLEDGMENTS

Hello Harries, I'm your newest member! A casual fan for years, I crossed over into superfandom while writing this book. Like millions of others around the world, now I too adore him. In fact, I recently met a friend for dinner at the famed Beachwood Cafe . . . and made sure we sat in Harry's booth!

ABOUT THE AUTHOR

Kathleen Perricone is a biographer with published titles about Marilyn Monroe, John F. Kennedy, Anne Frank, Barack Obama, Taylor Swift, Beyoncé, and dozens more. Over the past two decades, Kathleen has also worked as a celebrity news editor in New York City as well as for Yahoo!, Ryan Seacrest Productions, and a reality TV family who shall remain nameless. She lives in Los Angeles.

First published in 2024 by Epic Ink, an imprint of The Quarto Group,
142 West 36th Street, 4th Floor, New York, NY 10018, USA
(212) 779-4972 www.Quarto.com

10 9 8 7 6 5 4 3 2 1

ISBN: 978-0-7603-9319-2

Digital edition published in 2024
eISBN: 978-0-7603-9320-8

Library of Congress Control Number: 2024937135

Group Publisher: Rage Kindelsperger
Senior Acquiring Editor: Nicole James
Creative Director: Laura Drew
Managing Editor: Cara Donaldson
Editors: Sara Bonacum and Katelynn Abraham
Cover and Interior Design: Beth Middleworth
Book Layout: Danielle Smith-Boldt
Illustrations: Jessica Durrant

Printed in China